Biblical Keys to Maximize Your Marriage

How to Build a Heavenly Life with Your Spouse
Through Blessings and Difficulties

John F. Ramsey, Sr.

Scripture quotations marked (ESV) are taken from the ESV® Bible (The Holy Bible, English Standard Version®). ESV® Text Edition: 2016. Copyright © 2001 by Crossway, a publishing ministry of Good News Publishers. The ESV® text has been reproduced in cooperation with and by permission of Good News Publishers. Unauthorized reproduction of this publication is prohibited. Used by permission. All rights reserved.

Scripture quotations marked (KJV) are taken from the King James Bible. Accessed on Bible Gateway. www.BibleGateway.com.

Scripture quotations marked (NASB) are taken from the (NASB®) New American Standard Bible®, Copyright © 1960, 1971, 1977, 1995, 2020 by The Lockman Foundation. Used by permission. All rights reserved. www.Lockman.org.

Scripture quotations marked (NET) are taken from the NET Bible® copyright ©1996–2017 by Biblical Studies Press, L.L.C. All rights reserved. https://netbible.com.

Scripture quotations marked (NHEB) are taken from the New Heart English Bible. Edited by Wayne A. Mitchell. 2008–2022. Public domain.

Scripture quotations marked (NIV) are taken from the Holy Bible, New International Version®, NIV® Copyright © 1973, 1978, 1984, 2011 by Biblica, Inc.® Used by permission. All rights reserved worldwide.

Scripture quotations marked (NKJV) are taken from the New King James Version®. Copyright © 1982 by Thomas Nelson, Inc. Used by permission. All rights reserved.

Scripture quotations marked (NLT) are taken from the Holy Bible, New Living Translation (NLT), copyright © 1996, 2004, 2015 by Tyndale House Foundation. Used by permission of Tyndale House Publishers, Inc., Carol Stream, Illinois 60188. All rights reserved.

Scripture quotations marked (WEB) are taken from The World English Bible. Public domain.

Renown Publishing
www.renownpublishing.com
Biblical Keys to Maximize Your Marriage / John F. Ramsey, Sr.
ISBN-13: 978-1-960236-03-6

Praise for *Biblical Keys to Maximize Your Marriage* by John F. Ramsey, Sr.

Yet another example of Pastor John Ramsey using the talents God has given him to reach and teach those who listen to his words and take the opportunities to read and apply his writings in their lives. From humble beginnings to national prominence, his message has never changed, and his heart for those he serves never lessens. His books on singles, marriage, and family will help you take your relationships to the next level.

Dr. Al Long
Professor Emeritus, Indiana Wesleyan University

CONTENTS

Doing It God's Way!

When people are "in love," they believe they have all the answers. They think they don't need to listen to anyone else or even look at what God's word says about the institution of marriage. Hopefully this book you are about to read will dispel those notions and show you that God has a plan for what marriage is supposed to be. The world has distorted this plan. It sees the marriage bond as temporary, like the clothes you think you look good wearing one day and then get rid of at the next yard sale because you are tired of them and want a new outfit.

We all have heard about negative statistics and trends regarding marriage and divorce, but we don't often take time to break those numbers down and really assess what is happening in our society. The culture of today tells us many lies about how to live—that it is all about us and what makes us happy—and attempts to ingrain in us the mentality that if it feels good, we should do it. This mentality then shapes our moral conduct. The media bombards us with couples who live together without the marriage commitment or who jump from bed to bed, placing no value in monogamous relationships. Why should any of this surprise us when our society has strayed so far from God's plan for relationships between men and women?

The Bible says in 1 Corinthians 7:10–11 (NIV):

> *To the married I give this command (not I, but the Lord): A wife must not separate from her husband. But if she does, she must remain unmarried or else be reconciled to her husband. And a husband must not divorce his wife.*

How much clearer could God be? If everyone would simply take the time to read the entirety of 1 Corinthians 7 and take to heart what God has given us, the statistics would perhaps not be what they are. There would not be as much relationship trauma and unhappiness, and our society would be much better off than it is today.

As you read the chapters that follow, I ask you to look for ways to move your marriage to what God wants, rather than what the world tells you. If you choose to do things God's way, you will maximize your marriage. As God brings heaven into your home, you and your spouse will build a life that can withstand and thrive in seasons of blessings and difficulties.

Let God Yoke You to the Right Person

But since sexual immorality is occurring, each man should have sexual relations with his own wife, and each woman with her own husband. The husband should fulfill his marital duty to his wife, and likewise the wife to her husband.
—1 Corinthians 7:2–3 *(NIV)*

The following are some simple facts about marriage and the state of marriage in our society today. Ask yourself if you see yourself or your marriage in any of the statistics listed. If you do, then you are most likely experiencing marriage as hell rather than heaven.

- The average age of marriage for women in the United States in 2021 was 33.[1]

- The average age of marriage for men in the United States in 2021 was 35.[2]

- 60% of American adults believe they have a soulmate waiting for them.[3]

- 59% of marriages for women under the age of 18 end in divorce within 15 years. The divorce rate drops to 36% for those married at age 20 or older.[4]

- 60% of marriages for couples between the ages of 20 and 25 end in divorce.[5]

- 59% of adults ages 18 to 44 have lived with an unmarried partner.[6]

- Research indicates that people who live together prior to getting married are more likely to have marriages that end in divorce.[7]

- Children of divorce have a higher risk of divorce when they marry and an even higher risk if the person they marry comes from a divorced home. One study found that when a wife alone had experienced a parental divorce, her odds of divorce increased to 59%. When both spouses had experienced parental divorce, the odds of divorce nearly tripled.[8]

Isn't it amazing that although we know these facts, or at least find them unsurprising, we choose to continue down the path of a marriage from hell instead of pursuing heavenly marriage? Seeing what impact a failed marriage can have on children and their future marriages, how can we not try to find out how to make our marriages work? We should be doing everything possible to make our marriages as they were designed to be, rather than how the media tells us they should be. To do this, we must look at some of the issues that cause Christians and non-Christians alike to jump from relationship to relationship and throw their marriages away instead of committing to the godly covenant.

Of course, it stands to reason that if a marriage is going to be successful, it has to start out on the right path. Finding the person to share your life with is not like going to the store and picking out a new pair of shoes or going to the car dealership and picking out your next car. In today's society, this is the approach that many people take.

It never ceases to amaze me how many men and women get married to some person they have picked up in a bar or on the Internet and have not taken the time to get to know. Then they are surprised when a marriage that started out in hell comes to an abrupt end. As people shopping for shoes or a car imagine how they will look in the sharp shoes or the beautiful car, people shopping for a marriage romanticize how life will be with this new person who looks so good on the outside. Unfortunately, they do not take the time to know the inside.

KEPT BY GOD

During my junior year in college, God called me into the ministry. Within a year, I was teaching Bible studies on campus and preaching from time to time on Sunday mornings in local churches. I found that temptation does not stop because you accept Christ as your Lord and Savior, and

3

temptation did not stop just because God called me into ministry. In fact, the opposite might have been true. I am convinced that the enemy was angry that I answered the Lord's call with such fervor and conviction. Temptation intensified as I became more assured and more committed to following the path on which I knew God had placed me.

I had to make some serious decisions at the time. I knew that if I was going to be successful at living the life God planned for me, I would have to fortify my faith. Make no mistake about it: this was not an easy life to live. I was a young man determined to live right while being a student athlete and being pursued by women who knew me as such. It was not easy, but with God, *it was possible to overcome temptation*.

In God's word, 1 Corinthians 10:13 tells us that there is no temptation uncommon to man and that "God is faithful" and will always "provide a way out" if we choose it and really want to get out of a compromising situation (NIV). But you also need to know that God will not override your choice to sin.

A Christian must make a decision to live right and to remain celibate. Celibacy extends to activities such as foreplay, masturbation, and phone sex, just to name a few. Yes, even those things are excluded from a celibate life. The most difficult decision you will make in the fight against temptation is the decision to protect yourself from yourself. Nobody knew me better than I knew myself, so I had to make decisions that would not compromise my integrity or God's plans for my life. I had to make sure that I did not put myself in situations in which Satan had access to me or I would experience too

4

much temptation.

The first step in making the right decision was to be absolutely certain that I truly desired to be in God's will. While studying the Bible, I came across a scripture that I had heard many times as a church benediction: "Now to him who is able to keep you from stumbling..." (Jude 1:24 ESV). In that moment, this scripture was truly a revelation to me, and it became my way of life. I use this scripture to walk my daily walk. I realized that God was able to keep me; the catch was that I had to want to be kept.

The same holds true for you. God is able to keep you from falling if you are consistently determined to avoid falling and do not arrive unprepared at the moment when temptation arises.

At one point, I looked up and realized that it had been a year and God was still keeping me. I had not fallen prey to the tricks and attacks of the enemy. Now, this may not seem like much to you. But for me, a then twenty-year-old athlete on a college campus with many temptations, it was a huge achievement. God was teaching me how to live for Him. He was teaching me lessons I had to learn in order to go where He was taking me and continues to take me today.

Before I knew it, two years had gone by. Then three years had passed, and I graduated from college and started my first teaching job, preaching on weekends. Still, God was keeping me. Several years later, God called me to move to Indianapolis and start my first church. I was a single man serving God as a pastor, and He continued to keep me.

As a single person, I found that one of the most important

ways to overcome loneliness and depression was to remain active. The enemy wants to use your loneliness to draw you into various forms of temptation. As a believer in God, you should never put your life on hold for a relationship, whether you are male or female. When that person finally comes into view, you want to be clear about who you are as a child of God. This will better prepare you to become another person's partner in life.

After eight years of experiencing God's keeping power, I met my future wife. One of the things that motivated me most in meeting, knowing, dating, and ultimately believing in God's choice for my wife was that I had an incredible and blessed testimony to share with her about God's keeping power. With her trust and my knowledge of God, I would not compromise my integrity or hers. This enabled us to build a relationship grounded in godly principles.

You should know that in marriage, trust is everything. Making the right decision can lead you into a relationship that is wholly acceptable to you, your spouse, and God.

A SPOUSE ALIGNED WITH GOD'S CALLING

I would like you to be free from concern. An unmarried man is concerned about the Lord's affairs—how he can please the Lord. But a married man is concerned about the affairs of this world—how he can please his wife—and his interests are divided.
—1 Corinthians 7:32–34 (NIV)

This scripture leads me to conclude that God's will for the believer is to have undivided interests. This certainly does not mean that you shouldn't have a life outside of church and ministry, because it is important that we all live a balanced life. However, Paul's words indicate that the single years can be some of the most effective years in your life for getting involved in the things of God, such as choir and youth ministry. Single people must take advantage of that particular season of singleness and do as much for the kingdom of God as possible. There will come a time when the single person's concerns will shift to include those of marriage and his or her spouse, as they should. Married people have to, by necessity and design, divide their time between family and ministry.

The key to a successful life in marriage and ministry is to keep these respective interests and priorities in line. When God directs you and your spouse to each other, He is not bringing you together according to your common interests, but for a common purpose. Before you get emotionally involved with anyone, you must take an honest look at the person, asking several important questions about what he or she believes. Additionally, you must watch to see if the person's actions support his or her words. Though what the person says can be revealing, focus even more on observing what he or she does. Ask the following questions of yourself as well as the other person:

1. What do you believe God has called you to do?

2. Does this person's purpose fit into the context of what God is calling you to do?

3. Do this person's actions line up with what he or she claims to believe about God?

This is where things get sticky for many people. Usually, by the time people get this far, they have already met someone to whom they are physically attracted, and they have begun spending time with this person. Feelings are already developing. Along the way, they may see things that make them question the other person's sincerity and devotion to the things of God, maybe even the person's salvation. But because feelings are already involved, it seems too difficult to walk away at that point. It is important that you ask these questions up front, before you get your feelings invested, and carefully observe the other person's behavior from the beginning. Once emotional attachments form, many people go into denial. They hope the other person will change, or they try to change the person.

Perhaps you are lonely and simply thankful to have someone special in your life after a relationship drought. But it is critical to allow your wisdom to kick in so that you will not have to expend emotional energy, often negative energy, tolerating a bad relationship and, ultimately, a bad marriage.

BEING EQUALLY YOKED

Scripture tells us in 2 Corinthians 6:14–18 not to be unequally yoked with unbelievers. In order to have a deeper understanding of this passage, it is important to define *yoke*. A yoke is a type of harness that connects a pair of animals together to plow a field. In general, the yoke symbolizes some kind of burden you bear because of your responsibilities. A relationship with God in Christ eases our spiritual burden, which is why Jesus said, "Take my yoke upon you.... For my yoke is easy and my burden is light" (Matthew 11:29–30 NIV).

Now, you would never see a horse yoked together with a mule. The physical nature and temperament of a horse are different from those of a mule. If you yoke these two animals together, they will pull in different directions. Similarly, if you are in a relationship with someone who has not accepted Christ as Lord and Savior and has not chosen a godly life, or perhaps does not even believe in God, you can be pulled in the wrong direction. On the other hand, if a yoke ties two compatible animals together, it works as it should. Likewise, when you are yoked in the right relationship, with both people heading in the same direction, it should make your life easier, not more difficult.

It is amazing to me that people in love or with the idea of being in love always think that they can beat the odds of being successful in the wrong relationship. We must remember that when we are told not to be unequally yoked with unbelievers, it is a mandate, not just sound advice. Yet it never fails that some believers who know the truth about their unequal relationship will deceive themselves into believing that they can beat the odds. They reason that their relationship will work out despite all the evidence to the contrary.

A woman may tell herself, "I know he isn't saved, but if I get with him, I can change him." It is hard enough to change your own bad habits and actions, so what makes you think your witness is so profound that you can change another adult's behavior? It rarely happens. In trying to change another person, you will most likely end up frustrating yourself and the other person. People generally change only when they have a mind to change themselves. It is not worth the effort to try, given the costs and the risks. You may end up losing more than the hope of changing someone; you may end up losing the person as well as yourself and your God-given identity in the process.

Being in an unequally yoked relationship encompasses more than situations in which a believer is married to an unbeliever. Below are other examples of unauthorized or unwise relationships:

1. Both spouses are believers, but they have different levels of spiritual maturity. They may act and respond to similar situations in different ways.

2. The spouses have different goals and ambitions in ministry. They may have different calls in the work of God's kingdom.

3. You become involved with a person God has specifically warned you against.

4. You become emotionally involved with a coworker or anyone else of the opposite sex who is not your spouse. For example, if you are having reoccurring conversations with, text messaging, or thinking of anyone who is not your spouse or whom your spouse does not or cannot know about, you may be involved in an emotional affair. End it right away!

The wrong relationship will move you out of your place of purpose and dislodge you from your destiny. It will change your personality. You may start acting like that person rather than the person God created you to be. Remember that "bad company corrupts good character" (1 Corinthians 15:33 NIV).

All of your spiritual strength will go into making an unequally yoked relationship endure at a basic level of functionality instead of building a heavenly marriage. Trying to save your spouse or simply trying to survive the unequal relationship will end up being spiritually, physically, and emotionally unhealthy and unrewarding.

When you are in any wrong relationship, you have gone off track. In these cases, the enemy will go after your heart because you are controlled by your emotions. If the enemy can control your emotions, he can control you psychologically and physically. Relationship decisions should be made based on character and character development. Strive to live a life that gives testimony to your love of God, including in your decisions and relationships leading toward marriage.

Chapter One Questions

Question: Think about and discuss marriages that have been successful and have stood the test of time. What do you see in these marriages that you believe led to the success? Then think about and discuss marriages that have not worked. What do you see in those marriages that might have caused them to fail?

_____

_____

_____

_____

_____

_____

_____

Question: Do a quick assessment of your immediate and extended family. How many of your relatives have been affected by divorce? Based on the divorce statistics in this chapter, does your family reflect what others are doing, or does your family reflect God's plan?

_____

_____

_____

_____

_____

_____

_____

_____

_____

_____

_____

Question: Review the scriptures in which God shows us how to choose a spouse. If you are single, how do these Bible verses speak to you? If you are married, are you equally yoked? If not, what can you and should you do?

_____

_____

_____

_____

_____

_____

_____

_____

_____

_____

_____

_____

_____

Action: Find a couple that has been married for over twenty-five years and ask if you can sit and talk. Ask them specific questions about how their marriage has survived.

Action: Find someone who has recently divorced and ask him or her what caused the permanent split. Ask this person what he or she would have done differently.

Action: Search the Scriptures to see if God speaks to a marriage that has one believing spouse and one not believing. What does God say about this type of relationship?

Chapter One Notes

Your Choice, Your Destiny

This day I call the heavens and the earth as witnesses against you that I have set before you life and death, blessings and curses. Now choose life, so that you and your children may live and that you may love the LORD your God, listen to his voice, and hold fast to him.
—Deuteronomy 30:19–20 *(NIV)*

This passage of Scripture makes it clear that our decisions affect the quality of our lives. Our relationship decisions can cause us to spend all of our emotional energy coping with the results of those decisions instead of enjoying the fruit of marriage the way God intended. In Deuteronomy 30:19–20, God presented us with a multiple-choice question for our lives. Would we choose life or death, blessings or curses? God told us which answer to choose: life. He also told us why to choose this answer: so that we and our children would live and would love God, listening to Him and holding fast to Him.

We need to get back to the word of God and follow it to

be sure that our marriages are maintaining a heavenly perspective that can see them through hell. The more we trust in God and His word above our natural reasoning and expectations, the stronger our marriages will be in every season of life.

GODLY WISDOM FOR GOOD DECISIONS
ABOUT MARRIAGE

The Lord loves us so much that He has provided us with a guide to life that will direct our paths, protect us from making wrong choices, and give us the desires of our heart. We have access to this guide, the Bible, so why don't we simply make better choices? It is called free will. I often ponder this question during counseling sessions. I usually think, "Well, you had a choice in the beginning, my sister or my brother. Why did you pursue a relationship with this person and marry him or her if you knew you had serious issues from the beginning? God was already showing you the problems you would face, so why did you overlook them?"

I often say that couples think they can beat the odds. They truly believe that they can change someone else into the person they want him or her to be. They think they are so wonderful and will be so great that the other person will miraculously change for them. If he did not have a job when you married him, what makes you think he will become gainfully employed after you get married? If he had three children for whom he was not paying child support before he married you, what makes you think he will take care of your child? If she stayed at the club every weekend, hanging out with her friends, why would you think she would want to stay home after you married her?

It is important to acknowledge and accept a person simply and honestly for who he or she really is, rather than hoping, praying, and expecting that the person will eventually be different. A person will change only if he or she has a desire to change. If we were more honest with ourselves in the beginning, it would save a lot of heartache later on.

When couples come to me for counseling, I typically begin the session by asking them one question: "Do you want this marriage to work or not?" The answer they give usually determines the success of the counseling and can often predict the outcome of the marriage. Sometimes couples come to counseling as a last resort. Unfortunately, some couples come to counseling only because they are seeking permission for, validation of, or confirmation of what they already want to do: get out of the marriage. Their minds were made up even before they came in.

Reconciliation may be impossible if one or both of the spouses are unwilling to listen, grow, forgive, heal the hurts, and resolve their issues. However, with God, even the most desperate marriage can be reconciled if both people decide within their hearts to work on the marriage. Whatever you decide to do about your marriage, know that your thoughts and actions often determine the outcome, whether positive or negative.

The Bible says, "Death and life are in the power of the tongue, and those who love it will eat its fruits" (Proverbs

18:21 ESV). Many people make choices that they look back on with regret, wondering how in the world they got where they are. They say, "If only I knew then what I know now." Unfortunately, there are no do-overs in this life. But you can get it right this time if you are willing to pay attention and do things God's way.

When it comes to being single and believing God will lead you to the right mate, faith plays an important role in your decision-making. However, faith must accompany godly wisdom in order to make the right and the best choices for your life. Godly wisdom will keep you from allowing your emotions to make your decisions. Being guided by your emotions may cause you to make a permanent decision based on a temporary situation. It is unwise to base decisions for your life on how you feel at any given moment, because feelings tend to change over time, even from one day to the next.

You need to give yourself some time to make sure that what you feel is lasting and does not contradict godly wisdom. You may meet someone and fall in love after the first date. While love at first sight may be real, you need to slow things down to be sure that what you feel is consistent over time. Do not make a permanent decision about someone because you had a really good date.

Making a wise decision does not mean you have to become "spooky" with your faith. Spooky Christians feel the need to pray about every single decision in their lives, even if God has already given them wisdom in that area. They cannot enjoy the simple pleasures of life, such as socializing with friends or watching a ball game, without thinking those things are too carnal. Spooky Christians make minor decisions into huge ones. Before they can participate in any activity, they must take it before the Lord.

The Lord has given us good enough sense to know that if it is cold, we need to put on a coat before going outside. He has also given us enough intelligence to be able to decide for ourselves if chicken or fish would be the best choice for dinner. That said, there are many issues that should be taken to the Lord in prayer. One of those important matters is whom to date and, ultimately, whom to marry. God has certainly given us enough sense and words of wisdom to know that it is always unwise to date and marry an unsaved person. This was true even in Old Testament days, when Israel claimed and settled in the promised land. God, through His servant Joshua, warned His people not to intermarry with pagans:

> Or else, if indeed you do go back, and cling to the remnant of these nations—these that remain among you—and make marriages with them, and go in to them and they to you, know for certain that the LORD your God will no longer drive out these nations from before you. But they shall be snares and traps to you, and scourges on your sides and thorns in your eyes, until you perish from this good land which the LORD your God has given you.
> —*Joshua 23:12–13 (NKJV)*

Making wise decisions means that you must balance faith with the word of God to ensure that you are making the right choice. The Bible says that when God brought Eve to Adam, Adam said, "This is now bone of my bones and flesh of my flesh" (Genesis 2:22–23 NIV). Although God brought Eve to Adam, Adam did not have to choose her. Adam was a free moral agent with the ability to choose.

God has given us all free will. He wants us to be free to choose what we believe will make us happy, whole, and fulfilled, which means that we have the right to choose what we like. God provided Adam with the selection, but Adam was free to make the final choice. Interestingly enough, Adam did not see any burning bushes, the Red Sea did not part, the stars did not point to Eve, nor did any doves descend upon his shoulder. We should not always expect to have earth-shattering experiences that point us in the right direction. Sometimes God speaks in a quiet, still voice (1 Kings 19:12 NKJV).

Learning to make right, godly decisions is a matter of:

1. strengthening your relationship with God;

2. asking God to lead and guide your choices;

3. patiently waiting to hear from God, trusting that He will direct your life;

4. knowing that God has plans for you, that His plans are good, and that He wants the best for your life (Jeremiah 29:11); and

5. directing your heart in obedience to God's answer, even if it's an answer you do not like or understand at that point.

TRUSTING IN GOD,
NOT UNREALISTIC EXPECTATIONS

Trust in God is key when you are making decisions that have the potential to affect your life permanently, whether in a positive or a negative way. You should strive to choose a mate who will help you to achieve the great plans God has for you.

I want to turn your attention to the fact that the man is supposed to find his wife. Proverbs 18:22 states, "He who finds a wife finds a good thing, and obtains favor from the LORD" (NKJV). Please note that, although this may not be a scriptural mandate, God wants to give clear direction on the proper process for dating and relationships. By nature, a man needs to hunt, and a woman needs to nurture. If a woman is chasing a man, trying to make or convince him to love her, the relationship simply cannot work according to God's plans.

God does not intend for a woman to stalk her intended mate in order to have a relationship with him. The Bible doesn't say that she who "stalketh" a man finds a husband. She may succeed in wearing him down until he finally submits and commits. However, later on, she will grow tired of this one-sided relationship because this is not the way God intends marriage to happen. An overly aggressive woman may become less attractive to a man of character if he sees her as overbearing and dominating. In his mind, if she is overbearing and dominating before they get married, their relationship will continue to be like that afterwards. That kind of relationship is unattractive to a man, regardless of how beautiful he considers the woman to be.

When I was single and waiting on God to bring the right woman into my life, there were many women I could have chosen. However, I truly believed that God would give me the desires of my heart, and I was unwilling to compromise on what I believed God wanted for me. There were women who sought my attention or made themselves known to me, but in my mind, that was the wrong way for me to meet my future wife. There are many relationship books that tell women to be aggressive and assertive and teach them how to get their man. However, chasing a man to get him to submit to your will can only lead to an unhealthy relationship that will, more often than not, result in difficulty, heartache, and heartbreak. God provides the options, but we must make sure that the choices we make are in harmony with the principles of His word.

I have been in ministry for twenty-four years and in full-time ministry for eighteen of those years. It has always amazed me to find that many believers are balanced and levelheaded in the majority of their lives yet unrealistic in the area of choosing a spouse. I have had many men and women tell me, "Pastor, I don't want anyone who has children," yet they have several of their own. I have had women tell me that they want a man who is saved, has a good job, and makes a lot of money, but they themselves have bad credit, no savings, and a stack of unpaid or poorly paid bills. Men have told me that they want a woman who is a size two, but they are not exactly walking trophies.

The point I am trying to make is that we all have an idea of what and whom we want, but it's important to make sure that we are not setting ourselves up for disappointment by having unrealistic expectations. If you set yourself up with unrealistic expectations, you will be disappointed. Your Boaz may not come riding in on a white horse, ready to steal you away from your job, bills, and troubles. Stop watching soapy movies and start listening to the Holy Spirit. Yes, God has the ability to give you the desires of your heart, but it's also important to realize that, in fairness to everyone involved, you must work to become what you desire.

KEEP GOD ALONE AT THE CENTER

By *unrealistic expectations*, I mean expecting something from another person that you are unwilling or unable to give yourself. For example, if you are an unhappy person or have low self-confidence, you should not look for someone else to make you happy or to make you feel better about yourself. Happiness and self-confidence come from within. If you are waiting for someone to make you happy in order to be happy, no one will be able to fulfill that desire for you for an extended period of time.

Having that expectation is like trying to fill a bucket with a hole in it. The more someone fills the bucket, the more is required to fill it. If you are that bucket with the hole in it, over time, your mate will get tired of trying to fill the bucket, knowing that it's impossible to fill.

25

Having realistic expectations is an acknowledgment that no one is perfect and an understanding that we should seek to complement each other, rather than attempting to become whole as a result of being with someone. Expecting another person to make you whole is an unrealistic, unhealthy, and unreasonable expectation that no one could possibly live up to in the long term. I joke in sermons that some singles would have turned Jesus down because He had on dusty sandals and wore a shaggy beard. Would you have turned Jesus down because He did not look the part of the perfect man?

When you change your life to fit someone else's life or you make another person the center of your world, you are making that person your god. Allowing another person to become your reason for living puts too much pressure on him or her. If the attention you give this person takes your attention away from the things of God, you have made him or her your god.

You must ask yourself if you are allowing this new person in your life to draw you away from God and the things of God, such as daily devotional time, personal and group Bible study, participation in ministry opportunities, and worship services. You should also ask yourself if you are allowing this person to change your focus and your reason for existing. Have you begun taking time away from your ordinary responsibilities and the activities you previously enjoyed in order to spend time, perhaps unhealthy amounts of time, with this new person?

You must be honest and open with yourself. If you find that you are guilty of making that person the center of your life, it is imperative that you redefine the relationship and re-prioritize your life, with God as the head and your relationship with Him at the center.

MARRIAGE IS WORK

In Hebrews 13:4, God tells us that marriage is to "be held in honor among all" (ESV). Marriage was instituted and ordained by God for the lifelong relationship between one man as the husband and one woman as the wife. Why has our society, which not so long ago claimed, at least, to be Christian, strayed so far from this directive? At the heart of God's design, marriage is companionship, intimacy, and procreation. In the garden of Eden, God saw Adam's need for companionship, and He created Eve from Adam's rib. However, in today's world, we see over and over again an attack on the institution of marriage that God designed.

Genesis 2:18, 22, and 24 show us God's plan for marriage between a man and a woman. This simple and beautiful story is a blueprint for our lives, yet we allow things of the world to get in the way. We even allow our marriages to end in divorce when that is *not* God's plan.

The LORD God said, "It is not good for the man to be alone. I will make a helper suitable for him." ... Then the LORD God made a woman from the rib he had taken out of the man, and he brought her to the man. ... That is why a man leaves his father and mother and is united to his wife, and they become one flesh.
—Genesis 2:18, 22, 24 (NIV)

What is many times forgotten is how Christ and the disciples used the institution of marriage as a metaphor for Christ's relationship with the church. Understanding that Christ views this relationship as sacred and meaningful is reason enough for Christians to take the marriage covenant much more seriously than others do. Several times throughout His ministry, from the wedding feast at Cana to the Sermon on the Mount, Jesus used the institution of marriage to teach the basics of the kingdom of God.

If we examine the statistics of marriage and divorce and simply observe society, it becomes evident that the institution of marriage has been and continues to be under attack. Jesus said that "what God has joined together, let no one separate" (Matthew 19:6 NIV). How can we attack this trend and overcome issues that cause marriages to end?

Yes, I do know there are times when the Bible says that divorce is acceptable, but as you study these instances, you will see that they are specific situations. Being tired of a marriage from hell is not enough reason to toss it away. A healthy, lasting marriage requires work, sacrifice, and understanding from both the man and the woman. Think of *WORK* as an acronym that reveals what it takes to make and maintain a heavenly marriage:

W = Be *willing* to do what others won't and to work at making your marriage a heavenly one.

O = *Obey* God's word and His direction for what a heavenly marriage is supposed to be.

R = *Relate* to your spouse and listen to him or her. Continue to deepen the relationship.

K = *Know* your husband or wife and his or her needs and attempt to meet those needs.

As you go through the rest of this book, examine yourself and your life. If you are married, think about the WORK it takes to have a heavenly marriage. If you are not married, think about the WORK it is going to take to make sure that you are marrying the person God has for you. In all aspects of marriage, trust in God is fundamental. You have to work it out and walk it out on a daily basis.

Chapter Two Questions

Question: If you are already married, what did you learn from this chapter that you can apply to your marriage? If you are not married, how will you use these insights to help you find your mate? Whether you are married or single, what will you do differently tomorrow from what you did today after reading this chapter?

_____

_____

_____

_____

_____

_____

_____

Question: If you are single, what are you doing to ensure that God is keeping you as you wait for His direction regarding a marriage partner? If you are married, what are you doing to make sure that your marriage is a heavenly one rather than one going through hell?

_____

_____

_____

_____

_____

_____

_____

_____

_____

_____

Question: If you seem to be going through hell in a relationship, whether you are married or single, what is causing that situation?

_____

_____

_____

_____

_____

_____

_____

_____

_____

_____

_____

_____

Action: Find a married couple that seems to have a heavenly marriage. Spend time with them and talk with them about how they found one another and how they knew that God was in their decision to marry.

Action: Create a plan for steps you can take to show yourself and others that you are serious about a heavenly marriage. For example, you may refuse to watch TV shows that celebrate lifestyles that contradict God's plan.

Chapter Two Notes

CHAPTER THREE

How to Love

Wives, submit yourselves to your own husbands as you do to the Lord. For the husband is the head of the wife as Christ is the head of the church, his body, of which he is the Savior. Now as the church submits to Christ, so also wives should submit to their husbands in everything.

Husbands, love your wives, just as Christ loved the church and gave himself up for her to make her holy, cleansing her by the washing with water through the word, and to present her to himself as a radiant church, without stain or wrinkle or any other blemish, but holy and blameless.
—Ephesians 5:22–27 (NIV)

One of the problems in our society today is that too many people want to be married yet continue to function as if they were single. Many men fail to understand that until they make their wives a priority, their marriages will never get where they want them to be or become what God designed them to be. A husband must also understand that whatever goes on in his house is his responsibility, even if it is not his fault.

Women often fail to follow scriptural guidelines for marriage as well. They want to dominate the household and their husbands. They do not want to submit to the authority of God and the authority of the husband in the home. I suggest to you that it is time for men and women to get delivered from this video-game mentality, where everyone wants his or her own controller, and get serious about turning their marriages and families around to become what God designed them to be.

UNDERSTAND EACH OTHER'S NEEDS

Remember that Proverbs 18:22 says, "He who finds a wife finds a good thing, and obtains favor from the LORD" (NKJV). This text is powerful because it suggests that the benefit of God approving your selection is that He confirms His approval with favor! Finding the mate God intends for you will bring great favor from God and, therefore, happiness and joy. There will still be times when your marriage goes through hell, but with God's favor upon you and your spouse, how can your relationship fail?

In every relationship, it is critical that you learn to identify the needs of your mate and put yourself in a position in which you are more than able to meet those needs. At the same time, it is also critical that each party understands which needs are supposed to be met by the spouse and which are supposed to be met by God. If you do not learn how to differentiate between the two, you will put pressure on your husband or wife to meet needs that only God is capable of fulfilling.

An example of this would be self-esteem. Do not try to make your spouse responsible for your self-esteem. That is a need only God can meet. When you understand, through prayer and study of the Scriptures, how God values you as a person, it frees you from the pressure to be anything but yourself and keeps you from believing that it is your husband's or wife's responsibility to stroke your ego.

In Genesis 3:16, God said to the woman: "Your desire shall be for your husband, and he shall rule over you" (NKJV). A woman has two primary concerns: the family and security. Because she was made from the rib of man, her primary needs are met through a close relationship with her spouse. She feels a completeness when she and her husband are connected and their relationship is secure. It stands to reason that when the woman does not feel loved and connected, the marriage will not be what God intended. Likewise, when the man feels unloved and unconnected with his wife, the same tragic results can occur.

Knowing that marriage needs to bring the feeling of security and love, it is understandable that it may be hard for a woman to respect a man who says that he loves her but does not provide for her. How can a husband expect a wife to submit to what she cannot respect? I am not saying that all wants of each party are that important, but meeting the needs of the wife and family is the responsibility of the husband. He cannot expect his wife and children to respect him if he does not provide a safe and nurturing environment for them. It is hard, especially in the current economy, to provide adequately for a family, but in God's plan, this is the husband's responsibility.

PUT MARRIAGE ABOVE MONEY

I may anger some with this next statement, but it is my belief that it was not God's original design for the woman to have to work outside the home. My wife is a career woman, so I have nothing against women doing what they are gifted to do. My point is that I believe one of the reasons why so many marriages and families are functioning the way they are—or are not functioning and end in divorce—is that stress and constant pressure have become the norm because we have stepped outside of God's original design. We concentrate more on things of this world than on things of the next, and our worldly wants overcome our desire for a godly marriage and family.

You may be thinking I don't understand that your family cannot afford for the wife to be at home. I urge you to ask yourself if you have or desire so much stuff that it takes two incomes to sustain your family. If the wife desires to stay at home but cannot or the marriage seems to be in hell because of the stress of financial burdens or lack of time to care for and love each other, then it is time to fix that! You need to transition your family to a financial position that allows you to function with only the husband's income.

Please take the time to digest this fully before you reject the perspective I am offering. Even if the wife wants to work and have a career, think about how much less stress your family would be under if you could live your daily lives as if she were not bringing in money, because the second income is not imperative to paying the bills. I again state my belief that God's design is for the wife to be at home to nurture the family. If the wife works, it should be because both she and her husband desire her to have this job or pursue this career, not because the family needs her to work.

What can easily happen in a marriage is that the husband and wife forget to love one another and provide for each other's needs, because they get caught up in what they do rather than who they are and who they are supposed to be in God's eyes. The world tells us that we have to climb the ladder of success and that our wants are more important than our relationship with God. Jesus told Martha, "You are worried and upset about many things, but few things are needed" (Luke 10:41–42 NIV). If a husband and a wife have so much going on in their lives that they are missing the happiness and joy of one another, is it any wonder that many marriages end in divorce?

Even more importantly, if there is too much going on in their lives, they will miss the opportunity to enjoy the presence of God. Many Christians are like that even when they come to church. God's presence is all over the place, but they cannot truly experience it and benefit from it because they are so consumed with their schedules and everything they think they need to do that they miss God!

I am telling you that no matter what is currently happening in your life, your marriage is a treasure waiting to be discovered if you have not already found it. A loving marriage

39

is God's design. When both spouses understand this and follow God's plan, it's an awesome ride! Many times, husbands and wives let the concerns and desires of this world destroy what God has given us as a wonderful gift. Of course, money is one of these things that causes great stress in marriages and in other relationships. We let dollars or lack of them to dominate our lives and our thoughts, leaving little room for the joy of loving each other.

YOUR MARRIAGE IS BIGGER THAN YOU

Loving one another and having a strong marriage is important for many reasons, but in biblical terms, we need to understand that marriage is a model for the church. Because of this, it is safe to say that the condition of your marriage is bigger than you! A defective marriage affects the kingdom of God because when a family is weak, the church is weak.

For an example, we can look to Paul's letters to the church at Ephesus. He had established a church there and stayed for three years. The church was experiencing great growth and prosperity. Even so, Paul wrote to them to explain that to take the church to the next level, they needed to take their families and relationships to the next level. To further God's kingdom here on earth, husbands need to love their wives, and wives need to love their husbands.

If you are tired of going through hell in your marriage and are ready to make your relationship with your spouse a heavenly one, consider the following practical changes you can begin making today.

1. Respect one another and the roles God has laid out for each of you in His word.

2. Marriage requires mutual submission. It is impossible to be submitted if you are not willing to be accountable.

3. When your spouse challenges you, remember that a good mate is not out to hurt you, but rather to enhance you.

4. Wife, respect your husband. Few things discourage a man more than when his wife shows more respect for her friends, relatives, and coworkers than for him.

5. Husband, love your wife like Christ loves the church. Then you will be able to tolerate pain, and the object of your love will respond.

6. Tolerate trouble and resolve it. That is what it takes to restore a relationship. Christ was stripped and beaten, but He dealt with the embarrassment because He knew that change was coming.

7. If you love each other as Christ loves the church, neither of you will have to compete for time, because each of you will know you are a priority.

8. Understand that intimacy does not begin at night. It starts in the morning and lasts all day. Making love to one another is more than indulging in each other's body. Make yours an ongoing romance.

Remember that love is more than a feeling; it's a matter of choice and action. If you find yourself asking, "What if I don't love my spouse anymore?" the answer is simple: decide that you are going to love your spouse more!

It is not easy, but it is possible for a husband and a wife to love each other so much that their relationship can overcome the times when it goes through hell and become a heavenly marriage. This takes work on the part of both the husband and the wife and a constant cultivation of a loving, godly marriage to be successful. You have to make the conscious decision to love your spouse. Decide as a couple that you want to live your life together according to God's design and what is biblically right and discuss what this means.

Chapter Three Questions

Question: How do you show your spouse how much you love him or her? When was the last time you did something positive for your spouse that was totally unexpected? What was it? When you think about your spouse, what makes you smile?

_____

_____

_____

_____

_____

_____

_____

_____

Question: Did you ever observe your parents displaying affection for one another? How did that make you feel? Did you ever witness your parents fighting? How did that make you feel? What can you learn from their example?

_____

_____

_____

_____

_____

_____

_____

_____

_____

_____

Question: Why is it important for you and your spouse to model love for each other in front of your children and non-Christians?

_____

_____

_____

_____

_____

_____

_____

_____

_____

_____

_____

Action: Make a conscious effort to show affection toward your husband or wife outside the bedroom. Later, ask your spouse how it made him or her feel.

Action: Identify a couple in your life that has been married for at least ten years and ask them how they show love for one another.

Action: Ask your spouse what one thing you could do to make him or her feel more valued or to take a burden from him or her. Now do it!

Action: Commit to praying for your spouse daily.

Chapter Three Notes

Heaven in Your House

> But if serving the LORD seems undesirable to you, then choose for yourselves this day whom you will serve, whether the gods your ancestors served beyond the Euphrates, or the gods of the Amorites, in whose land you are living. But as for me and my household, we will serve the LORD.
>
> —*Joshua 24:15 (NIV)*

All of us, at one time or another, have wondered why we do certain things or act a certain way. I want to attempt to explain why certain types of behavior patterns exist within many of our families.

THE SINS OF THE FATHER

The Bible declares that the sins of the father are visited "upon the children to the third and fourth generations" (Exodus 20:5–6 NKJV). I suggest to you that there will come a time in your life when you have to fight your daddy's devil!

If you do not realize this and fight that devil, your marriage will most likely not be a heavenly one. Take some time now to examine yourself and your family.

- If you can look at your family and see several generations of pregnancy outside of wedlock, I want to suggest to you that it's not just an act; it's a spirit.

- If you can look at your family and see several generations of addiction, that's not just an act; that's a spirit.

- If you can look at your family and see several generations on welfare, I want to suggest to you that it's not just a difficult time; it's a spirit.

- If you can look at your family and see a lack of education, I want to suggest to you that this is also a spirit. I once knew a family that had five kids, and not one of them graduated from high school. You must know that ignorance will limit your personal potential!

- If you can look at your family and see several generations of lazy and irresponsible men, I suggest to you that it is a spirit. If the head is out of place, the rest of the family is dysfunctional!

What I have found is that many families continue in these cycles because they do not come to grips with the fact that there are problems in their homes. They believe it is normal, so they do not make the changes necessary to have happiness, joy, and abundance in their lives. You see, when it comes to sin, I have discovered that as long as you like what you do, you will never change what you do. Many people and families go through cycles of sin because they do not really want to give it up. Here is my little saying about the sin in some families and homes:

> They do it.
> They regret it.
> They repent of it.
> The guilt leaves.
> They repeat it!

How do you fight this tendency to repeat the sins of those before you? One of my favorite statements is: *When it comes to deliverance, persistence will distort resistance!* Being purposeful and persistent will allow you to overcome bad habits and destructive patterns from your past and allow your home to be different.

THE VALUE OF A GODLY HOME

Why is it important to have a godly home and a heavenly marriage? Jesus said, "How can anyone enter a strong man's house and carry off his possessions unless he first ties up the strong man? Then he can plunder his house" (Matthew 12:29 NIV). This text implies that when you and your household are bound up in sin, the enemy can do what he wants to your family and your marriage. You must persistently clothe yourself in God's word and have the Holy Spirit in your life and your home.

How can you make this transition and bring about lasting change in your marriage and family? What I have found in my years of ministry is that what you do not appreciate will depreciate. In other words, if you want to have a heavenly marriage, you must work on it constantly and spend time every day in affirmation, thanksgiving, and prayer.

Over the last twenty years, I have seen the devil intensifying his attack against the institution of marriage and family. One of the ways he begins to erode the fabric of the family is by causing spouses to fail to appreciate what God has given them. I am not talking about material possessions here, but about the gift of each other and the gift of children.

Let me give you a personal illustration. A friend of mine gave me an expensive watch on a special day. This watch's value is not only in its material worth. I value it because of when it was given, how it was given, and the person who gave it to me. This watch has lasting personal value to me because of my love for the person who gave me the gift. I treasure it and take care of it, and it brings me joy. I tell you this story because this precious gift given to me can symbolize the precious gift God has given you: your spouse.

Remember that "he who finds a wife finds a good thing, and obtains favor from the LORD" (Proverbs 18:22 NKJV). If God has given you a spouse, He has given you a gift of much greater value than the watch given to me. You have a responsibility to value, protect, and appreciate the gift God has given you. If you don't, your relationship will depreciate, just as my watch would if I were to stop taking care of it properly.

REAL LOVE BRINGS SOME
HEAVEN TO YOUR HOUSEHOLD

Many people simply do not know how to show appreciation for their marriages and families and how to care for them properly. We all need to understand that:

- Just because you are married does not mean that you know how to be married.

- Just because you have had sex does not mean that you know how to make love.

- Just because you have children does not mean that you know how to be a parent.

- Just because you make money does not mean that you know how to handle it.

What I have seen is that, to a great degree, we have become Christians in a materially driven, individually focused culture. We are so caught up in trying to provide for the house that we fail to spend time with the people in the house. We need to realize that real love is the desire to give benefit to others, even at our own expense. What I see many times in marriages that end up in hell is that lust has taken over and the relationship is ruled by the desire to benefit oneself at the expense of others. That will quickly bankrupt the marriage and family.

God gives us direction and mandates as far as our homes

are concerned. When Jesus was giving His disciples an example of how to pray, He said, "Our Father in heaven, hallowed be your name, your kingdom come, your will be done, on earth as it is in heaven" (Matthew 6:9–10 NIV). Based on this prayer, we can see that it is the will of God for us to experience heaven on earth. This means that God expects there to be some heaven in our households. Through the Scriptures, He also gives us all the direction we need to be sure this is possible in our marriages and families. The enemy knows all of this and will try to destroy a marriage and tear down a home any chance he gets.

One of the things I like to show people is Ephesians 5:25–33. Let me break this down for you as a metaphor for how spouses should love one another. In this passage, Paul compared the love a husband should have for his wife to Christ's love for the church. Christ gave up His own life, sacrificing Himself out of love. He cares for the church as part of His own body, as a man should care for his wife. Though the church is not perfect, Christ will work to remove the spots and blemishes, just as we should work on our marriages.

God also said, "I will never leave you nor forsake you" (Hebrews 13:5; Deuteronomy 31:6 ESV). Christ gave of Himself, His very life, when we had nothing to offer Him (Romans 5:6–8). In these ways, God has modeled for us how we are supposed to be present for and committed to our spouses.

SIX REQUIREMENTS FOR A
SUCCESSFUL MARRIAGE

In order to have a heavenly marriage, spouses must understand each other's needs. Let me share what I believe each of the two spouses needs for a successful marriage. The woman needs:

1. Communication

2. Honesty

3. Financial support

4. Family commitment

We have touched on each of these, and I believe them to be paramount to a heavenly marriage. The man is a bit simpler. He needs:

1. Sex (Sorry, ladies, but it's the truth.)

2. Praise

No matter what you, your spouse, and your relationship have been through, you can make your marriage into a heavenly one. All you need to do is look to Noah to know that it is possible. If a man can build an ark when it is not raining, take all the criticism from family and friends, weather the greatest storm in history, and come out of it with his marriage and family intact, then how can we say that it is not possible for our marriages and families to be successful? It is possible, and it's time to start putting in the work to make it happen.

Chapter Four Questions

Question: What is the difference between a house and the home?

_____

_____

_____

_____

_____

_____

_____

_____

_____

_____

Question: Do you know a family you believe to have a heavenly home? What makes this family so special, and how can they serve as an example?

_____

_____

_____

_____

_____

_____

_____

_____

_____

_____

Question: How can spouses be lovingly held accountable for their biblical roles in the family?

_____

_____

_____

_____

_____

_____

_____

_____

_____

_____

_____

Question: Husband, knowing what your wife needs, how will you treat her differently? Wife, knowing what your husband needs and what God directs, how will you treat him differently?

_____

_____

_____

_____

_____

_____

_____

_____

Action: Characterize your family as an inanimate object. For example, you might think of the family as a house with additions to it. While different parts of the house are of different ages and sizes, all have the same foundation. Similarly, the family grows from a marriage to a couple with children. While the family may change over time, the belief in Christ as Lord and Savior should remain the foundation. What did you learn from this activity?

Action: Make a list of what you believe are the attributes of a heavenly home. Then make a list of your family's attributes. In what ways is your household a heavenly one? Where is there room for growth?

Chapter Four Notes

_____

_____

_____

_____

_____

_____

_____

_____

_____

_____

_____

_____

_____

_____

_____

_____

_____

_____

CHAPTER FIVE

Until Debt Do Us Part

Money certainly makes the world go 'round, and it can also make even the most in-love couple split apart in hurtful ways. I have seen this happen many times in my marital guidance practice because Christians are in no way exempt from allowing money issues to creep into their marriages. Money is guaranteed to be a point of stress until an agreement is reached.

Let's face it: it is hard to have family stability if you do not have financial stability! The number one reason divorces occur in America is financial hardship. Most arguments in marriages are over money. Therefore, if we can bring stability to our finances, this will help to bring stability to our marriages.

In *The Millionaire Mind*, Thomas Stanley surveys thousands of millionaires to understand how they live, what they believe, and to what they attribute their success. Here are some of the principles these millionaires follow in their lives:[9]

1. Be honest with all people.

2. Be well-disciplined.

3. Have a supportive spouse. (Most of these millionaires have been married to the same woman for twenty-five years or more.)

4. Work harder than most people are willing to do.

5. Love your career.

6. Be well organized.

7. See opportunities others do not see.

8. Live below your means.

9. Have a strong religious faith!

While we do not need to be millionaires to have heavenly marriages, these principles provide useful guidance as we seek to establish and maintain financial stability for our families.

COUNT THE COST AND BE PREPARED

Before Jesus fed five thousand people, He told the disciples, "Have them sit down in groups of about fifty each" (Luke 9:10–17 NIV). This indicates that there must be order before there can be increase. Planning and preparation are essential to the financial aspects of your marriage. Jesus said:

For which one of you, when he wants to build a tower, does not first sit down and calculate the cost, to see if he has enough to complete it? Otherwise, when he has laid a foundation and is not able to finish, all who are watching it will begin to ridicule him, saying, "This person began to build, and was not able to finish!"

—Luke 14:28–30 *(NASB)*

This text shows us the importance of preparation for the life you and your spouse (or future spouse) are building. You cannot build anything without tools. The tools for financial stability include wisdom, knowledge, and information. These tools contribute to our understanding of our financial situation and how to manage and improve it.

Proverbs 8:18 says, "With me are riches and honor, enduring wealth and prosperity" (NIV). "Me" in this context is wisdom. Lack of preparation and understanding will keep you from being able to complete what God has called you to do, but financial preparation based on godly wisdom leads to security.

Security brings comfort to a woman, and financial problems threaten her security. Eve did not need to have a job in order for her and Adam to get by. As I said in a previous chapter, if you and your spouse are living on two incomes, you should make it your goal to adjust to living on one income instead.

Of course, our ultimate security comes from the Lord. In Luke 12:22, Jesus said to His disciples, "Therefore I tell you, do not worry about your life, what you will eat; or about your body, what you will wear" (NIV). God wants us to trust and rely ultimately on Him, and He gives us wisdom to handle our finances in a responsible way.

THE VIRTUOUS WOMAN

Typically, in the church, when we talk about a virtuous woman, we are referring to a spiritual woman. However, a virtuous woman is also a balanced woman. She is what I like to call "the total package." She knows not only how to operate spiritually, but how to operate practically as well.

Proverbs 31:10–31 outlines the characteristics of a godly woman. It sets the standard for what a woman should aspire to be and shows a man what to look for in a woman. As you read this Scripture passage, you will see that this woman's skills far exceed domestic abilities. This is a woman who understands how to make money, keep money, invest money, and spend money.

In verse 10, "virtuous" (NKJV) is also translated "of noble character" (NIV). If you have a virtuous woman, you should be able to trust her with money. Do not go into a relationship with someone who does not know how to handle money, because at some point, this dysfunction will affect you! Regardless of who handles the money, both parties should be aware of the state of their finances. If you were to die, your spouse should know how to access the money and understand the system you used to handle the money.

Proverbs 31:10 goes on to say that "her worth is far above jewels" (NASB). A good woman should be treated in a way that she feels valuable, and a virtuous woman can be beautiful and happy with herself however little she has. She understands that God made her beautiful, with beautiful skin that protects her from the environment, eyes that can see His world, and ears that can hear His word. Recognizing your natural beauty is the first step toward realizing that you do not need the most expensive perfume or a membership at the country club to make you valuable and worthy. Stop pretending to be someone you are not and living on a level that does not reflect your actual earnings. Scale it back. Live on your level and enjoy your life by simply being you.

Verse 11 indicates trust in the relationship. Trust is the foundation of a good relationship, especially in the area of money! The woman of Proverbs 31 is investment-minded (verse 16). She invests in real estate in addition to being a business owner (verse 24). She does whatever it takes to complete the task in front of her (verse 18), and she is in shape as well (verse 17). She is a giver and helps people in need (verse 20).

This woman and her husband "have no lack of gain" (Proverbs 31:11 NASB). In other words, she knows how to take what she has and make it increase. Verse 13 says that this woman "works with her hands in delight" (NASB). She is diligent and enjoys what she does! When you have a bad attitude in your work, those around you pay for it. Proverbs 12:24 says, "Diligent hands will rule, but laziness ends in forced labor" (NIV). Lazy people always end up making somebody else rich.

The woman of Proverbs 31 is dressed for success (verse 22). She is not simply taking care of a man, but contributing to what her husband is already doing (verse 23). She does not live in fear, because she is prepared (verse 21).

SMALL BEGINNINGS AND GOOD STEWARDSHIP

The best place to start is to observe how you and your partner spend money on little things. Do you wait for a good deal or make spontaneous decisions? Do you have the mentality of "I deserve this," or is your mindset more in the ballpark of "I've worked for this, so I'm going to treat myself this one time"? An occasional splurge isn't bad, but if you and/or your spouse views money and possessions as a means to happiness, then you are in for a rough future!

If you are looking to get married, pay attention to how your potential life mate handles money. Does she have an expensive purse but no money in it? Is he driving a flashy car but borrows from you to pay for gas? Is he or she saving for retirement? Does he or she have a plan for emergency situations? Watch out for the little things because they can point to much bigger problems under the surface.

Zechariah 4:10 tells us, "Do not despise these small beginnings" (NLT). What this says to me is that we need to live within our means. Wife, when you have a husband who is providing for you, make sure that you are functioning within the boundaries of his ability to provide. Getting caught up in the mentality that you need to keep up with what other people have will lead you to live beyond your means, which will cause stress in your marriage. The pressure of financial instability will come into play, and the marriage relationship will suffer. It is not in God's plan for you to live beyond your ability to pay for the way you live. If you do, no matter how much money comes through the door, more will go out.

Even if there is plenty of money coming in, there is never a justification for wasting it. God's word tells us that we are to be good stewards of what He provides and not use it frivolously. In my years of service, I have seen many people gain great wealth only to squander it on meaningless toys and activities. They make money the center of their lives and relationships rather than having God at the center, and they end up with nothing. There are also examples in the Bible of men and women who seemed to have it all yet fell because they lost direction for their lives. They began to concentrate on things of the world instead of the things of God, and it led them off course.

In order to follow a life of financial stewardship and achieve financial stability, you need to plan for it. You need to work for it. You need to put a strategy in place and stick to it. But sometimes marriage messes that up. When two people with different financial goals come together, it can prove to be problematic. You and your spouse (or potential spouse) must come to an agreement on finances and how to handle them. Only then can you both move forward into a life of sound financial decisions and good stewardship of what God has given you.

Chapter Five Questions

Question: If you are married, do you and your spouse agree on how to handle finances? Has there ever been any financial issues that caused conflict in your marriage? If you are single, are you being intentional about how you handle your finances?

_____

_____

_____

_____

_____

_____

_____

_____

Question: Whether you are married or single, are you preparing for the life you want to build? What additional information might be helpful as you put together a strategy for meeting your goals? Do you pursue godly or worldly wisdom when it comes to finances? Are there any changes you need to make to come into alignment with godly wisdom regarding money?

_____

_____

_____

_____

_____

_____

_____

_____

Question: Are you living according to your means? What specific changes can you make to stop overspending and start saving?

_____

_____

_____

_____

_____

_____

_____

_____

_____

_____

_____

_____

Action: Seek out resources, training, books, and other tools that will help you to come up with a plan for handling your finances according to godly wisdom.

Action: If you are married, have a discussion (or series of discussions) with your spouse to make sure that you both are on the same page regarding your finances. Come to an agreement on budget, spending, and goals. Make sure that you both are equally informed on all financial matters. Create a plan to get your finances in order and a strategy to achieve financial stability. If you are single, create a budget and a plan for how you want to handle your finances going forward.

Chapter Five Notes

CHAPTER SIX

Children—Blessing or Burden?

Jesus said, "Let the little children come to me, and do not hinder them, for the kingdom of heaven belongs to such as these." When he had placed his hands on them, he went on from there.

—Matthew 19:14–15 *(NIV)*

In my years in the ministry, I have seen and heard many reasons for people to feel that their marriage is in trouble and going through hell instead of being the heavenly life together they were expecting or hoping for. All the reasons for the tragedy of divorce are disturbing, but the most disturbing to me is when children are involved and sometimes blamed for problems in the marriage.

Before I go any further, I want all who read this book to understand that children belong to God and we are only their caretakers. The sooner we comprehend this truth and internalize our responsibility and privilege to take care of God's precious gifts, the better off we will be. It never ceases to amaze me how some people do not understand the blessing of children. They look at raising children as a burden. Just the other night, on our local news, there were at least three new stories of how children were abandoned, lost, stolen, abused, or even killed by those who had been entrusted with caring for them. I know that we are not supposed to feel wrath toward others and that God will handle punishment for unconfessed sin, but when I hear about and see grown men and women mistreating children, it goes to the core of my soul. How any human being can treat a child in that manner is beyond my comprehension.

If a couple comes to me and begins to tell me how their children are causing the problems in their marriage, I have to bring them quickly back to the word of God. I lead them to the understanding that God loans us His children and we are to be their caretakers. A good scripture to remember comes from Matthew 18. Jesus made it very clear that we have a serious responsibility as parents, and there are dire consequences for not meeting this charge.

> *Whoever receives one little child like this in My name receives Me. But whoever causes one of these little ones who believe in Me to sin, it would be better for him if a millstone were hung around his neck, and he were drowned in the depth of the sea.*
> **—Matthew 18:5–6** *(NKJV)*

All who believe their children to be a burden in their marriage should dwell on Christ's words and think long and hard about the ramifications of not caring for the gifts their heavenly Father has given them.

Please don't misunderstand. I know that raising children is tough. Sometimes you may dream of how life will be once the kids are out of the house and on their own. That's normal, and the tough times are not fun to go through. However, it is our duty and responsibility to raise our children in a loving, caring home and not let them believe that they are a millstone around our necks, lest we end up with one around ours.

At this point, you may be thinking, "It's evident that he just doesn't understand. He hasn't had to raise our kids." No, I haven't had to raise yours, and I don't want to, but my wife and I are raising ours. I can speak with some authority regarding the challenges of raising three very unique children. You will have the chance to learn more about them a little bit later.

THE BLESSING OF A BLENDED FAMILY

Another issue I see is when a couple has a blended family—that is, when one or both spouses have children from previous relationships. It does not matter what the situation was with the previous relationships: divorce, the death of a spouse, or a child out of wedlock. Blended families can be very difficult to navigate, and sometimes a marriage quickly goes to the hell side because of these issues if they are not addressed prayerfully and directly. No matter how the children came into the family and what the family structure looks like, they are still God's children, and we have the command to provide for them and lovingly raise them to adulthood.

If there are children in the home who are not biologically yours, you may sometimes get frustrated and feel that these children are not your responsibility. That is not the case! Once the marriage takes place, those children are your responsibility under God's word, and you are to love them and cherish them as your own. You are to direct them and guide them. A perfect example of what you are to do can be seen in Joseph, Jesus' earthly father. Can you imagine if your wife came to you and told you the story that Mary told Joseph? What did he do? He trusted God and trusted Mary, and he raised Jesus as his own, in love. What a powerful example for us to follow!

You may be thinking, "But Pastor, you don't understand how frustrated I get with these kids and how frustrated they get with me. It seems to spiral out of control until we all get exasperated!" If you have a blended family and you find yourself at a point where you are thinking, "These aren't my kids, so why do I have to worry about them?" remember what we established at the very beginning of this chapter. No children are ours. They belong to God, and we are their caretakers. In Ephesians 6:4, God's word gives us this command: "Fathers, do not exasperate your children; instead, bring them up in the training and instruction of the Lord" (NIV). Whether the children in your home are your biological children or not, you are still to love them and not frustrate them or get frustrated with them.

THE BLESSING OF OUR FIRST CHILD

You may sense that I am passionate about children being a blessing and not a burden. Perhaps you can understand why when I tell you about my own family. I am blessed in many ways, and one of my greatest blessings from God is the children He is allowing my wife and me to nurture into adults.

We are not what most would call a normal nuclear family. God has blessed us, and we have chosen to celebrate diversity in our family. God is at the center of my life, and my wife and children are the center of my world. The ministry revolves around them; I do not make them revolve around the ministry. I tell preachers all the time that we do not want our children to grow up resenting our calling to full-time ministry. I believe this resentment happens when children grow up seeing their daddy going to great lengths to meet the needs of the congregation but not taking the time to attend their games and other events. Why should they want to serve a God who took their parent(s) away from them? It is hard to explain to a ten-year-old why his father or mother has time for everyone and everything but him.

Before we got married, Alicia and I never really discussed the number of children we wanted to have. My wife is the oldest sibling of four, with no sisters, and I am the youngest of five, with both sisters and brothers. I knew that I didn't want five children, and she didn't want four, so I think it was unspoken between us that two was the magic number. After one year of marriage, we were ready to start our family. I imagined we would have two healthy children, preferably a boy and a girl. My son would love sports like I do, and my daughter would be a "girly girl" like her mother. I saw myself working hard and giving my family the things I never had growing up. I knew that I, like my older brothers, would be an involved, "hands-on" father with both of my children. Today, I am blessed to have three beautiful, vivacious, and unique children. Each one has brought something different to our family because they each entered our home differently.

Our first son, John Jr. (aka Johnny), was born healthy, handsome, and full of personality. Our second child, Jeremiah David (aka Jay), was diagnosed in utero with a series of serious health challenges. Jeremiah's journey is a book of its own. I cannot wait to share the joy that this handsome, artistic young man has brought into our lives. Our third child, "the chosen one," is a daughter named Judah Maree (aka Juice). She was adopted at birth and quickly took over my heart with those big, beautiful, dark brown eyes. Are my children a blessing or a burden?

I remember when my wife went into labor with our first child like it was yesterday. I had been smiling on the inside ever since the first ultrasound that confirmed our child was a boy. The feeling of seeing your wife give birth to your first child cannot be fully described with words. My son, whom we named John Fitzgerald Ramsey, Jr., was born on October 11, 1997. Alicia, who is not overly spiritual in the slightest, told me that God confirmed the name when she wasn't sure about it. The Lord told her that if she named our son after me, he would double all of the accomplishments I achieved in life.

Now let's fast-forward to 2011. My wife and I were already beginning to see the manifestation of what the Lord had told her regarding John Jr., our "son #1." He looked just like me, he wore glasses like I do, and he had to fight for his academic success as I did. At the age of thirteen, his athletic ability was already prodigious and exceeding my own.

I began playing football when I was six years old. I knew early on that I would excel at football and track because I loved the game of football and I enjoyed running. The discipline I showed from a young age for working out and studying the game was uncommon. As a senior at Snider High School in Fort Wayne, I had the privilege of being recruited by several top athletic programs. I accepted a full ride to Miami of Ohio on a football and track scholarship.

I share this background with you because we soon began seeing similarities in our oldest child. John Jr. started playing football at the age of six, and he also began taking tae kwon do. He started winning sparring matches in local competitions, and by the age of ten, he had received his black belt. Johnny won the national tae kwon do championship in his age bracket at the age of ten, the first such win for the KTA studio led by Master Cottee. He also received MVP for his football travel team due to his scoring ability and exemplary sportsmanship.

John Jr. and I were both excited when track season started in the sixth grade. This would be his first time running track, and I couldn't wait to see the similarities he and I shared in our running styles. At the first meet, I could see in his stride the confidence he held while running against eighth graders.

It was amazing how I could see myself in his facial expressions and mannerisms before he participated in his event.

By the time John Jr. entered the seventh grade and could play football for his school team, he was prepared, and he dominated in various positions. He was already catching the attention of the high school, and he wanted to excel in all positions, something I never had the opportunity to do. In my eyes, my first son certainly accomplished double what I had in his middle-school years.

Seeing his athletic ability at such a young age caused me great joy, and it also caused a change in my work schedule because I wanted to help shape his athleticism. That meant I needed to take him to his practices, attend his competitions, and stay in communication with his coaches.

Parenting was designed to be a partnership. Alicia and I agreed that when one parent redirected a child or gave consequences, the other parent needed to support the decision. Johnny found out very early in life that there was no point in running to one parent to try to undo what the other parent set in place. Whenever he came to me with a request, I automatically asked, "What did your mother say?" If he hadn't already asked her the same question, he knew that I would not make a decision until she and I agreed on it.

The Bible states in Proverbs 22:6, "Train up a child in the way he should go, and when he is old he will not depart from it" (NKJV). By the time John Jr. was a preteen, he knew the flow of our family and how decisions were made regarding his best interest.

THE BLESSING OF A CHILD WITH SPECIAL NEEDS

When our first son was two years old, we decided we wanted to have another child. My wife had just started her Master's in Education program, so we decided to let it happen when it happened. The birth of a second child changes the dynamics of a home, but you are aware of how it works since you have "been there, done that." This was not the case with our second child, because we found out at twenty-five weeks of pregnancy that our second son would be born with some serious health challenges. Jeremiah David was born on July 31, 2001, the same weekend we opened New Life Worship Center. We did not share any information with family or friends until after Jeremiah was born. We were told that he had an enlarged left kidney and a hole in his heart. The most dismantling news was that he was missing his corpus callosum.

The corpus callosum is the part of the brain made up of millions of nerve fibers that connect the left hemisphere of the brain to the right hemisphere.[10] Jeremiah's corpus callosum was partially there or not there at all. We were told that he might be a college graduate or he might have extreme mental retardation. We would have to wait and see.

At that point in our lives, Alicia and I had a healthy, rambunctious two-year-old son and a baby boy born extremely ill. We brought Jeremiah home from the hospital unaware of what the future held for him and our family. We were introduced to a new world of doctors: a cardiologist, a urologist, a genetics expert, a pediatrician, a neurologist, and an assortment of therapists. In the beginning, all of this was very difficult for me to digest. How was I, as a man, a husband, and a father, to handle the pressure that comes from having a child with special needs? I dove into getting the new church up and going, which caused me to be less visible at home. When I reflect back on those first three years, I now see that it was my way of dealing with having a sick child. I wanted to work so that I could provide the best quality of life for him.

My wife handled all the doctor appointments, medications, and childcare. I didn't often see her break down, but I found out later, as the years passed, that she did have such moments but chose to have them alone. At first, I wanted to try to fix what was happening with my family. That's how I am wired. If there is a problem with my wife or my children, I will try to fix it. Well, I could not fix this. All I could do was trust God and support my wife.

There were many days when I broke down and cried like a baby. I asked, "Why, God? Why my son?" I cannot say that I got an answer, but I do know that Jeremiah is taking my faith in God to a level that I never dreamed possible. Alicia and I must "walk by faith, not by sight" (2 Corinthians 5:7 NKJV). We stand daily in Hebrews 11:1: "Now faith is confidence in what we hope for and assurance about what we do not see" (NIV).

As the years progressed, we shared more with family regarding Jeremiah's diagnosis. We were also very open with our church about our son so they could pray for us to understand the developmental delays that he began to display. At the age of two, he could not walk or talk, and he did not have any teeth. Therapists came to the house to work with him through the state's early childhood development program called First Steps. Jeremiah captured the hearts of everyone because he loved to be held and he loved to kiss. My wife took great pride in making sure that our kids looked nice.

At the age of three, Jeremiah had his first grand mal seizure. This type of seizure can kill you if it is not stopped with the rectal medication. I remember the first seizure Jeremiah had because it was on a Sunday morning. My wife was awakened by Johnny, who carried Jeremiah downstairs, which was unusual. Jeremiah was not making any noises. Johnny had seen his brother awake in the room and carried him downstairs. When Alicia saw that Jeremiah was not responding to her voice, she began to pray because she knew something was wrong, and she called 911. She had been researching Jeremiah's disability on the internet weeks prior to this episode and learned that many of the children have seizures. When she noticed Jeremiah's abnormal response, she knew that was the problem.

I was able to make it home right after the ambulance left the house. They had accidentally left my wife, so she was there to tell me, "Go back to preach. The devil is not going to get the victory. Our son will be fine. Go do what God has called you to do."

I don't know how I did it, but I did go back and finish the services that day. Jeremiah left the hospital with medication to control the seizures, and we left with a new level of faith because his seizures were connected to sleep. This meant we had to pray that God would keep our son asleep so he would not wake up in a seizure. There were countless times when Jeremiah just so happened to be in our bed and would wake my wife or me with his twitching or the slight clicking noise his mouth made during a seizure. We immediately began praying and followed the action plan the doctor gave us. We praise God that our son had to go to the hospital emergency room only three times in his first nine years of life.

You may be thinking that after the seizures began, Alicia became a stay-at-home mother, but she did not. Her way of staying balanced was to work full-time, and she had great health insurance, which allowed us the best quality of care for Jeremiah during those early years.

When you are raising a child with special needs, medical expenses can be a substantial burden on the family. We saw my wife's medical insurance and my secondary insurance as a blessing. In addition, we were able to afford a full-time caregiver so that Jeremiah would not have to attend day care and the therapist could come to our home to work with him. We are a team when it comes to Jeremiah's care!

We decided that as God continued to bless us, we would make sure that Jeremiah was exposed to many different opportunities in his life. He has been to Disney World numerous times, been on two cruises, and seen every major gospel recording artist (he loves gospel music). He has flown to California, Texas, and New York. We have given him every therapy that will benefit him and help him to become a productive citizen in life. We know that if we do everything we can in the natural world, then God will do the supernatural and complete the healing in Jeremiah's body.

My wife and I share parenting responsibilities so that neither one of us becomes overwhelmed. Statistics show that parents with special-needs children have a higher divorce rate than the national average. Many people sacrifice their purpose and calling when they have a child born with special needs. I believe this causes great tension in the marriage and resentment in the home. Alicia and I determined to do what we could to keep our family well-balanced. We found a non-profit organization called National Disorders of the Corpus Callosum that has connected us with families that have children with the same disability. Once a year, we attend their conference as a family vacation so we can meet new families and go to workshops to learn more about Jeremiah's condition.

My wife and I had to realize that we couldn't do it all by ourselves. We needed to leave room for God to send us help, and we needed to learn to accept the help He sent. Even with Jeremiah going to school for a time, my mother and three other ladies helped us with the children. They called themselves "Team Ramsey." This support allowed my wife and me to have date nights, attend conferences without the children, and go to Johnny's athletic events.

THE BLESSING OF AN ADOPTED CHILD

You may be wondering, "Why in the world would they adopt a child when they already had such busy lives and a special-needs child?" Well, we often asked ourselves the same question before we made the final decision to adopt. In 2005, my wife began talking to me about adopting a little girl. She spoke about it often during our marriage, but I did not see how we could do it. To be honest, I shut down the idea by asking if she was going to stay home full-time with the kids. She was not ready to do that, so the conversation would end. As time went on, we continued with our careers and parenting our two boys. Alicia no longer discussed the idea as she progressed in her career. The church was growing, and I was becoming interested in other ministry opportunities. Our life was good, but it was not complete.

In 2007, I had a friend in town who shared stories with me about being an adoptive parent. He and his wife were also parents of a special-needs child. I remember talking to him about my wife's desire to adopt, and he encouraged me to do so. He told me how his special-needs son matured when they adopted younger siblings. I hadn't seen it from that perspective before. He told me, "There will never be a great time to do it. You just have to do it."

After that conversation, I encouraged my wife to consider moving forward with adoption, but this time she had reservations because she did not see how it could fit into our new lifestyle. I was now the pastor of a church, with multiple services several times a week, and she was a principal. She did agree that we should do some investigating, so we sat down with an adoption agency to find out how it all worked and if it was something we really wanted to do. We hesitated again when we found out the difficulty of having a sex-specific adoption, because we knew we wanted a daughter.

At this point, it was 2008, and the adoption plans were

once again on hold. In October of each year, Bishop Dr. I. V. Hilliard has an annual conference in Houston, Texas, that my wife and I attend. This particular year, Alicia took a couple of days off work so she could attend the conference with me for the entire time. One evening, while we were at a dinner hosted by Bishop Hilliard, we were sitting at the table with a lady we did not know. She used to work for a well-known female evangelist and was now working in her family church. She was very kind and enjoyed talking to my wife about her family.

During the conversation, I left the table, and when I returned, my wife had a very strange look on her face. She told me to sit down so she could share what this lady had said to her. The woman had seen me minister on The World Network, and she remembered me speaking about our special-needs son. My wife confirmed that it had been me on the broadcast. The lady began to talk about how Jeremiah's testimony was going to make a great impact for the kingdom of God and in our ministry. She went on to ask about our daughter.

When my wife told her that we didn't have a daughter, she said that we were supposed to. She said that our daughter would do something special in the life of our son with special needs and something special for us. I always tell our congregation that prophecy is confirmational, not directional. This prophecy was confirmation, and we immediately began the adoption process when we returned to Indianapolis.

We decided to use a smaller adoption agency, and the doors began opening right away. We were chosen by a birth mother who was due in March of 2009, but my wife and I agreed that was too soon for us. Then we were selected by a second birth mother, but she wanted an open adoption with visitation, and that was something we didn't want. Alicia and I were amazed. We had heard of people waiting for years to be selected by a birth mother or going overseas because they could not connect with a birth mother here. There we were, new to the process, and within the first six months, we were selected by not just one but two birth mothers. We later discovered that there were not many African American families adopting through private agencies. Most adopted through families or the foster care system.

As we entered the summer of 2009, my wife and I sat down to talk about her transitioning out of her career into a full-time position at the church. My wife is not a stay-at-home type of woman, which is fine with me. When I met her, she was working two jobs, so I knew from the beginning the type of work ethic she had. Having her work with me at the church would give her more flexibility, would be a great help to me in the ministry, and would help us to keep the balance in our family with the addition of a new baby. She was hesitant, but she knew it was a must in order for us to expand our family and keep up with the boys' hectic schedules.

It was a difficult decision for my wife to make after fifteen years in public education, but with my support, she willingly sacrificed her demanding career for our family. I find myself ministering more and more about selflessness in marriage and in parenting. You cannot be both selfish and a good parent. It is no longer about *you* and what *you* need or want. You need to think in terms of *we*!

Alicia submitted her letter of resignation in July of 2009. The next month, we received an email informing us that another birth mother had selected us. She was only forty minutes away and already had three children; this would be her fourth. I remember the phone call we made from my church office. After we spoke with the young lady, she decided she wanted us to adopt her child, and we scheduled a time for us to meet.

We decided to incorporate Johnny and Jeremiah in our decision to adopt. Johnny was honest and said that he didn't know how we would handle Jeremiah and a new baby. It was hard for him to process his mother not working sixty hours a week anymore and having more time for another child. We thought that if we took our sons with us to meet the birth mother, that would help them to understand the process of adoption. We showed Jeremiah pictures of babies and talked about it a lot in the present tense.

It was a Saturday in October when we drove as a family to northern Indiana to meet the young lady who was carrying our soon-to-be little girl. We spent time talking with her about herself, her children, and her current living situation. We agreed to a semi-open adoption. There would be no visitation, but my wife would send pictures and updates periodically. At first, our family and friends did not understand this type of adoption, but they soon realized it was a blessing because this openness gave my wife the opportunity to learn about the family history and attend doctor appointments. The birth mother told the social worker that she knew we were the right family because we showed concern for her as well as the unborn child. The birth mother was so touched by our communication and concern that she invited us to be in the delivery room. She told my wife that she felt more like a surrogate mother, and she was happy to give us our "little princess."

On January 7, 2010, around noon, my wife got the call that our little girl was on the way. This was unexpected because the baby was not due until late January or early February. My wife had a beautifully decorated room (pink everything) and a closet full of clothes, but no car seat. Indianapolis had just been hit with the first real snowstorm of the season, and Alicia rushed out in the storm to purchase a car seat. We both packed clothes and headed to the town where the birth mother lived so we could be close to the hospital.

It was a false alarm, but we ended up staying at a hotel for three days because my wife did not want to take a chance on missing the birth of our daughter. The birth mother felt comfortable calling my wife directly, so my wife updated the social worker on the process as we waited in our hotel room for our baby to arrive.

On January 9, 2010, around 1:00 p.m., they induced labor, and our daughter was on the way. We hung out in the delivery room with the birth mother and her sister. It was a very pleasant environment. You would never have thought that the young lady on the delivery table was about to give her baby away to people she had met only three months prior. It did feel as if she were carrying our baby for us, because there were no signs of sadness. When it was time to push, my wife held one leg while I waited outside the door. My wife told me that the young woman had to push only three times before our daughter came out.

Judah Maree Ramsey was born on January 9 at 6:30 p.m. When the doctor asked whom to give the baby to first, the birth mother said, "Her mom," and pointed to my wife. I know it sounds like a movie, but this is what happens when God makes your divine connection. I then came into the room, and I must admit that when I saw Judah, tears poured out uncontrollably because it was unbelievable to me. We had a healthy, beautiful daughter.

The hospital was adoption friendly and allowed my wife to stay there to care for Judah. I returned home after one night to spend time with the boys and bring them to the hospital to see their mom and new baby sister. Johnny later said that he wasn't sure about adopting a baby, but when he saw her in the hospital, he didn't want to leave her.

The birth mother did not give our baby another name; she allowed us to name her. She asked to see the baby only once before she left the hospital so her children could meet the baby. It was such a divine connection that everyone, including us, is amazed at how much Judah looks like my wife and younger son.

I forgot how much work it would be for my wife after we brought Judah home. I felt like even though she was there, she was not there. She could not attend church for six weeks, and the baby took all her attention.

Some people asked why we did not try to have another birth child. They wondered if we were afraid that another child would be born with health challenges. That was not the case for my wife and me. The process of adoption was a blessing for our family and many other people as well. We decided to give a baby girl a life she could not have had with her birth mother: a Christian home, financial stability, two parents, and brothers who love her dearly. We live our life as an open book so our congregation can see that children are blessings and that God blessed us with the opportunity to extend our family in this special way.

The Blessing Beyond the Burden

Are children a blessing or a burden? If you believe them to be a burden, then you need to go to God's word, examine what your responsibility is, and rid yourself of those thoughts. If you believe, however, that children are a burden in a positive sense, then you truly get it. This may seem confusing, but what I mean is that the burden is a blessing!

This is not double-talk; it's the truth. God says that you have a burden—that is, a responsibility—to raise in love the children He places in your care, and this burden should be considered your blessing. Many married couples long to have children but cannot. If God has blessed you with the burden of children, whether biological or not, take the blessing and thank Him each day for the opportunity to care for the wonderful gift He has given you.

Always remember that with the gift God has provided, there comes a responsibility to obey God and teach His word to the next generation:

He decreed statutes for Jacob and established the law in Israel, which he commanded our ancestors to teach their children, so the next generation would know them, even the children yet to be born, and they in turn would tell their children. Then they would put their trust in God and would not forget his deeds but would keep his commands.
—Psalm 78:5–7 *(NIV)*

So, are children a blessing or a burden? In a marriage from hell, there is only a burden. However, in a heavenly marriage, the answer is *both*. One of the greatest blessings of a heavenly marriage is God granting us the burden of raising His children.

Chapter Six Questions

Question: How do you affirm your children? How do you show your children that they are loved? Do you do this based on who they are and what they truly need, or are you focused on how you think love should be shown? How do you celebrate the unique characteristics of each of your children?

_____

_____

_____

_____

_____

_____

_____

_____

Question: Do you give your children specific responsibilities? If so, how do you set goals for your children in their responsibilities to the family? If not, evaluate what responsibilities you can begin entrusting to them.

_____

_____

_____

_____

_____

_____

_____

_____

_____

_____

Question: How do you model a heavenly marriage for your children so they will be able to apply your example to their own marriages? Are there areas where you need to improve?

_____

_____

_____

_____

_____

_____

_____

_____

_____

_____

_____

Action: Evaluate your discipline strategy. In what ways does it resemble the way God, our heavenly Father, disciplines us? Are there any changes you need to make to achieve the desired results? If so, write an action plan with specific steps and goals to reshape how you approach discipline.

Action: Assess if you are regularly encouraging your children in their faith walk. If you are neglecting this aspect of parenting, create a strategy to make it a daily part of your life with your children. This will help to guide them in their own relationship with Christ.

Chapter Six Notes

Adultery—Impulsive Choices, Long-Lasting Consequences

One evening David got up from his bed and walked around on the roof of the palace. From the roof he saw a woman bathing. The woman was very beautiful, and David sent someone to find out about her. The man said, "She is Bathsheba, the daughter of Eliam and the wife of Uriah the Hittite." Then David sent messengers to get her. She came to him, and he slept with her. (Now she was purifying herself from her monthly uncleanness.) Then she went back home. The woman conceived and sent word to David, saying, "I am pregnant."

—2 Samuel 11:2–5 (NIV)

With recent media attention focusing on celebrities and their marriage failures and indiscretions, it would be remiss of me to avoid a discussion of the dangers associated with unauthorized, illicit, and immoral relationships. We live in a very sensuous society. As followers of Christ, we are to be in the world but not of the world (John 17:14–16). The world wants us to walk in gray areas where the lines between right

99

and wrong are blurred and a person justifies his or her actions based on personal feelings. Operating in gray areas can lead to satisfying fleshly desires and emotions, but we must stay faithful to God in singleness and marriage because there is no pain-free ticket for admission into fornication and adultery.

Nothing can destroy a family faster than the act of adultery. The only difference between the public relationships featured in the media and the ones everyday people are having is that the former are being played out publicly for everyone to see, read about, and judge. If I could ask these celebrities one question, I would ask, "Was it worth it?" I feel sure that most of them would admit that the cost—loss of relationships, personal and public embarrassment, loss of respect—was not worth the momentary pleasure they experienced from their decision to be unfaithful to their spouses and families.

ADULTERY DEFINED

I am reminded of a public official who, for months, denied having a relationship with a young intern. When he was called upon to answer whether he had engaged in an improper relationship with the woman, he replied, "I have had no sexual relations with that woman." Interestingly enough, how he defined that relationship is a problem many people experience when they have so-called friendships with individuals outside of their marriages. Is sharing intimate conversations appropriate? Is doing everything except engaging in "the act" appropriate? Is it appropriate to share a long hug? What about a kiss? Are any of these actions considered adultery?

The Bible is clear as to the answers to these questions, so let's take a moment to define several terms that are relevant to this topic and examine what God's word tells us about them.

Adultery is defined as "voluntary sexual intercourse between a married person and someone other than their lawful spouse."[11] Jesus expanded the definition of adultery to include an allowance for and cultivation of lust (Matthew 5:27–28).

Lust is defined as an "intense or unbridled sexual desire."[12] In the context of Christian life, it can be described as the desire for anything that is contrary to what God wants us to have (Galatians 5:17). To *tempt* is "to entice to do wrong by promise of pleasure or gain."[13]

An *unauthorized relationship* can be defined as any relationship that you feel you cannot be open about with your family and friends. If you feel a need to lock or hide your phone, erase text messages, or go to another room when having a conversation with a "friend," you may be involved in an inappropriate, dangerous, unhealthy, and sinful soul tie.

Soul ties can be healthy or unhealthy. An *unhealthy soul tie* is an ungodly, perverted relationship that keeps you from being free to become all that God intends for you to become. The soul is made up of the mind, will, and emotions. When you talk with someone about your hopes and dreams, difficulties, disappointments, frustrations, joys, and sorrows, you are actually relating on a soul level. If you are regularly communicating with a person other than your spouse about the issues of life, you are developing an unhealthy soul tie that may cause problems in your marriage over time.

If you have a strong desire to talk to a person other than your spouse about your life, your concerns, your problems, and your victories, you might have established an unhealthy soul tie and be involved in an emotional affair. If you feel the need to hide the true nature of your relationship from your family and friends, you may be engaged in an unauthorized relationship, even if the relationship is not of a physical nature. Affairs do not have to be physical to be sinful and dangerous. Sometimes coworkers or friends start out having innocent conversations that end up taking them down a path of destruction they neither anticipated nor wanted.

The enemy wants your heart! He tempts you to try to lead you away from God's will. He goes after your heart because he knows that most people are controlled by their emotions and their desire to satisfy their flesh. The devil knows that if he can control you emotionally, he can control you physically. Decisions that are made during emotional times and times of crisis have the potential to cause irreparable damage to even the strongest of marriages.

Song of Songs 2:15 warns, "Catch for us the foxes, the little foxes that ruin the vineyards, our vineyards that are in bloom" (NIV). A look, a joke, a touch, or an inappropriate conversation has the potential to start something that may compromise the integrity of the marriage. We must guard ourselves and our hearts against anyone or anything that may compromise the marriage and undermine the vows of love taken on the wedding day. There is never any room for

compromise in the kingdom of God. Small foxes can spoil the
vine of love.

You must ask yourself, "Is any relationship outside of my
marriage worth me losing my family, my dreams, and my
goals?" Your reputation, security, and dreams can be de-
stroyed overnight because of one decision for fleeting carnal
pleasure that you thought no one would ever find out about.

As you may recall from the Scripture passage at the beginning of this chapter, David made a decision to summon
Bathsheba without any thought to the consequences. His decision was based on the emotions and desires of the moment.
He paid no thought to Bathsheba, his own position of power,
his past or current successes and blessings, or the consequences of his actions. His thoughtless decision to act on his
feelings caused an unexpected and unwanted pregnancy,
pain, grief, guilt, recrimination from a friend, and the death
of Bathsheba's unsuspecting and innocent husband, who
served David loyally in battle. Despite everything else we
know about David, it is apparent that during this time, he
acted with selfishness and spiritual immaturity.

In Matthew 5:28, Jesus said that "whoever looks at a
woman to lust for her has already committed adultery with
her in his heart" (NKJV). With that first look (the small fox),
David had already committed adultery. We are living in a
time when it seems that few people possess the ability to control their flesh. The Bible says, "Walk in the Spirit, and you
shall not fulfill the lust of the flesh" (Galatians 5:16 NKJV).
Being spiritually mature means having the ability to exhibit
self-control and godly wisdom in every situation.

THE LIES OF THE ENEMY

The devil wants to trick you into thinking that none of the repercussions that adulterers face will happen to you. The trick of the enemy is to make you think that you are too smart to get caught. It won't go down like that for you. You are way smarter than everyone else.

Secret sins may escape the eyes of your family and friends for a season, but God sees and considers all of your acts. He has a heavenly camera shining light on your actions. No matter how smart you think you are, your sins will find you out. Numbers 32:23 says, "But if you fail to do this, you will be sinning against the LORD; and you may be sure that your sin will find you out" (NIV). It is foolish to think that because no one knows about your secret sin, God will turn His head and overlook it. When we choose to sin, it will eventually and invariably lead to destruction if we do not repent.

We should avoid even the appearance of and opportunity for impropriety in dealing with members of the opposite sex. Have you ever found yourself doing any of the following?

1. Having work meetings off-site with a member of the opposite sex.

2. Getting personal advice or personal counseling from a member of the opposite sex.

3. Talking to a member of the opposite sex about your marriage, concerns, or problems.

4. Allowing work conversations to extend too long.

5. Looking forward to conversations before work, at lunch time, or during breaks or finding reasons to stop by someone's office or desk to say hello.

6. Looking forward to sitting beside the same person in meetings.

7. Looking for reasons to contact the person after hours to discuss work-related issues.

8. Tolerating flirtations, seeking or enjoying praise from a coworker, or telling or listening to and enjoying inappropriate stories and jokes.

9. Receiving or sending inappropriate emails or text messages.

10. Riding to meetings together, just the two of you.

11. Calling the other person to check up or check in and see how he or she is doing.

12. Serving as a mentor, friend, or Big Brother or Sister to the child of a single parent without your spouse's knowledge, approval, or input.

While these may be totally innocent acts, we must avoid putting ourselves in situations that compromise our integrity or that may lead anyone else to believe something about us that is not true to our nature as Christian men and women.

Why Would Anyone Be Unfaithful?

Sometimes we look at others and wonder why anyone would cheat on his or her spouse. This is especially true when we look at people who live in the public eye and seem to have everything anyone would want: a great career, money, fame, and a beautiful or handsome spouse. When people cheat on their spouses, they may feel perfectly justified in their own minds because they do not feel the same way about their spouses anymore, their spouses are not around enough, or they feel that they are not spending enough quality time together. It seems to me that if you can find the time to cheat, you can find time to spend with your spouse.

Let's return our focus to David and consider his situation. David went from being virtually unknown to being very well-known. He went from a humble job in obscurity to a great job that put him in the public eye. The enemy has a way of targeting successful people, because if he can get successful people to fail, then people who look up to them will also be affected by their failure. In Revelation 12:4, God's word says, "And his tail swept away a third of the stars of heaven and hurled them to the earth" (NASB).

There are several reasons why people look for gratification outside of their marriages:

Selfishness or narcissism. In some cases, individuals want what they want without regard for their spouses and families. When selfishness, arrogance, and ego take hold, people are unlikely to think of how their choices will affect someone else. Once desire takes root and the opportunity presents

itself, without God's help, people may even convince themselves that they have a right to pursue this sinful relationship
and will proceed without further thought to the consequences. Deciding to have an affair is a selfish personal
choice. No one can force you to have an affair regardless of
what you believe someone has or has not done. If you have an
affair, you are exercising your free will to make that decision.

Time and opportunity. There are certain seasons when the
enemy intensifies his attacks against our lives. We must be
careful to avoid sedentary lifestyles and idleness. When we
have too much time on our hands, the enemy has an opportunity to infiltrate our minds with useless, distracting, and
inappropriate thoughts. The enemy will set you up if you are
not careful to avoid placing yourself in compromising situations. For example, why was Bathsheba taking a bath on the
roof? I have found in my studies that in ancient Palestine, the
roof was used as a sitting or resting place. It is possible that
Bathsheba had an agenda when she went on the roof to bathe
that night? If she had avoided taking a bath on the roof in the
first place, she would not have been seen by David. However,
if David had refused to linger there, watching a woman taking
a bath on the roof, he would not have compromised his integrity. He could have gone back to bed instead. Even better,
he could have gone to battle with his army instead of sending
them on while he stayed home. In this moment, David failed
to see how his one act of disobedience would bring destruction and negatively impact every aspect of his life. We can see
in 1 and 2 Samuel that David's impulsive decision to sleep

with Bathsheba caused one disaster after another, including rape, murder, and revolt. Oh, those long-lasting consequences!

Lack of appreciation for what they have at home. The old adage that "the grass is greener on the other side of the fence" can come into play when people are tempted to stray from their marriages. This misguided perception often leads men and women to seek fulfillment from extramarital relationships. If you have ever had a lawn, you know that it thrives when you water and tend to it. An overall lack of appreciation for what is at home will open the door for adulterous relationships. The Bible says that it is important to "rejoice in the wife of your youth" so you may enjoy continued blessings (Proverbs 5:18 NIV).

Boredom. An often-cited complaint about marriage is that one's spouse becomes boring and the relationship loses its excitement. When people become bored, they lose their mental edge. As a result, their minds lead them into places where they should not wander. We must take our bored and sinful thoughts captive (2 Corinthians 10:4–5) and stop the sin before it festers in our hearts and minds. One way to avoid boredom in the marriage is to continue seeing the good in your spouse. You should also begin dating your spouse again. Find ways to reenergize and rebuild the marriage in ways that work for both of you. Dating your spouse has to become a priority, because life's pressures and troubles have a way of overwhelming couples that are not intentional about and committed to keeping the marriage alive and exciting.

The thrill of secrecy. Secrecy can be an attractive part of the overall fantasy of an affair. For some, sneaking around to create opportunities for a fling is as fun and erotic as the relationship itself, and the thrill of not getting caught is its own reward. This type of thinking can lead only to destruction.

Affirmation of their self-image. Men may seek the chase and the challenge of an affair to affirm that they still have what it takes to attract a woman. A man may feel the need to validate his success in life beyond his job. In some cases, if a man does not feel successful in his professional life, he may seek success in other areas, including chasing women, to affirm his self-image. Women, on the other hand, have a need to feel loved, appreciated, and valued. If a woman feels inadequate in any way, she may look outside the marriage to affirm her self-image. A woman may be enticed to have an extramarital affair if a man tells her repeatedly the things her husband is not telling her at home. Her male coworker may make her feel admired and beautiful. His words are tricks of the devil designed to encourage her to sin against the marriage vows.

Mid-life crisis. Sometimes when men and women reach middle age, they look back over their lives and wish they had done more or something different. People in their forties, fifties, and sixties may fear growing older and may believe that they have missed out on some important aspects of life. They may feel like failures in certain areas and attempt to recreate or spice up their lives by having affairs or engaging in other dangerous or age-inappropriate acts.

Hanging out with unmarried friends or married friends who cheat. The likelihood of someone being unfaithful to his or her spouse increases when he or she has a lot of unmarried friends or friends who glamorize cheating on their spouses. Hanging around spouses who cheat makes cheating seem like the "norm," so it is important to befriend as many happily married couples as possible.

ADULTERY HAS CONSEQUENCES

Regardless of the reason for engaging in relationships outside of one's marriage, it is sin and will not go unpunished. Always remember that adultery may start sweet but will always end in bitterness. The Bible has much to say about adultery and the consequences for those who commit adultery:

- "You shall not commit adultery" (Exodus 20:14 NIV).

- "But why should you be captivated, my son, by an adulteress, and embrace the bosom of a different woman?" (Proverbs 5:20 NET).

- "He who commits adultery with a woman is void of understanding. He who does it destroys his own soul" (Proverbs 6:32 NHEB).

- "You have heard that it was said, 'You shall not commit adultery;' but I tell you that everyone who gazes at a woman to lust after her has committed adultery with her already in his heart" (Matthew 5:27–28 WEB).

- "Let marriage be held in honor among all, and let the marriage bed be undefiled, for God will judge the sexually immoral and adulterous" (Hebrews 13:4 ESV).

- "With eyes full of adultery, they never stop sinning; they seduce the unstable; they are experts in greed— an accursed brood!" (2 Peter 2:14 NIV).

- "So I will cast her on a bed of suffering, and I will make those who commit adultery with her suffer intensely, unless they repent of her ways" (Revelation 2:22 NIV).

You may be thinking that I do not understand your situation. It is different for you. All of these scriptures and ramifications are right on for everyone else, but not necessarily for you. If this is what you are thinking, I am here to tell you that it simply is not true. The sin of adultery is like being dead. If you are dead, you are dead. You cannot be any more or less dead. It is the same with adultery. There are no levels or degrees. If you have committed adultery, then you will pay the consequences. You can choose your sinful act, but you cannot choose the consequences of your decision. Our selfish choices impact those who come after us, even to the third and fourth generations.

When couples stay together after adultery, adultery can be forgiven but is never forgotten. Adultery scars reputations and brings distrust, ill will, bitterness, and resentment. Adultery may lead to divorce, which breaks up marriages and families. Divorce breaks hearts and shatters dreams. It deprives children of a sense of financial and emotional security and well-being. It leads to the sale of the family home and expenses involved in maintaining two separate households for mother and father. It often leaves women and children in lower states of financial stability than men.

This leads children to think that the divorce was somehow their fault. Children lack full-time access to noncustodial parents, and relationships between noncustodial parents and children often suffer. This causes distress in children that can affect their future relationships.

Adultery and divorce also affect relationships with extended family and friends, who must choose avoidance, defense, or rationalization. Sometimes a spouse leaves the marriage to marry the person with whom he or she had an affair, but I find that marriages beginning in adultery are rarely successful.

In light of these consequences, you must ask yourself: Is adultery worth it? Is a momentary thrill or pleasure worth the unraveling of the family relationships God has given you? The time to ask these questions is *before* you start down a path that may lead to an inappropriate relationship or an unhealthy soul tie. You cannot control other people, but you can control your own thoughts, words, and actions. Instead of looking over the fence, start tending your own lawn. Then you may find the grass on your side of the fence getting greener and greener.

Chapter Seven Questions

Question: David was described as a man after God's own heart (1 Samuel 13:14; Acts 13:22), so how could he allow himself to fall into the trap of adultery? Do you know any David-like people in your own sphere of influence? Are there ways in which you relate to David? What can you learn from his example?

_____

_____

_____

_____

_____

_____

_____

Question: What does the Bible tell us we are to do if we find ourselves in a compromising situation—for example, if a coworker begins to discuss personal issues with us, puts us in situations in which we feel uncomfortable, or tells us off-color jokes or stories?

_____

_____

_____

_____

_____

_____

_____

_____

Question: Has an adulterous affair affected your own family or extended family? What were the effects on the individuals involved in the affair, their spouses, their children, and others? What does this reveal to you about why God desires us to flee from this type of temptation?

_____

_____

_____

_____

_____

_____

_____

_____

_____

_____

_____

_____

Action: Think of a celebrity who has recently been caught cheating. What have been the ramifications of that adulterous act or relationship?

Action: Make a list of people, situations, and sins that tend to trigger temptation in you. Come up with a plan, including relevant Bible verses, to help you avoid these temptations as much as possible and resist them when you do face them.

Chapter Seven Notes

CHAPTER EIGHT

Forgiveness—
Learning the Art of Letting Go

Brothers and sisters, I do not consider myself yet to have taken hold of it. But one thing I do: Forgetting what is behind and straining toward what is ahead, I press on toward the goal to win the prize for which God has called me heavenward in Christ Jesus.
—Philippians 3:13–14 (NIV)

One of the greatest challenges that couples face is in the area of forgiveness. God is so serious about forgiveness in the life of every Christian that He gave the mandate so we would know why forgiveness is important: we must forgive other people in order to receive forgiveness from God (Matthew 6:14–15; Luke 6:37). God also gave us a model, Jesus Christ, so we would know how we are to forgive.

Learning how to forgive your spouse early in your marriage will set the stage for how happy, whole, and healthy your marriage will become as the years progress. The earlier

119

couples learn to forgive, the more easily correction and reconciliation will become the norm in the marriage relationship.

KEEP NO RECORD OF WRONGS

Spouses find it difficult to forgive one another because they are often guilty of keeping mental records of each other's sins and the times they have been hurt by the other person's words or actions. We are all required to forgive, even and especially when we do not feel like it. Many times, couples find it difficult to forgive because they keep adding each unkind word or inconsiderate action on top of the last one until the stack of offenses becomes so large that the marriage crumbles under its weight.

First Corinthians 13:5 says that love "keeps no record of wrongs" (NIV). You and I have been called to reflect the image of Christ in everything we do, and that includes forgiving people who hurt us. I don't know what they did to you, but I do know what not forgiving them can do to you.

Refusal to forgive, sometimes known as *unforgiveness*, holds you hostage to the memory of the offense. Unforgiveness often does more damage than the initial hurt because it keeps you bound to what someone did to you in the past. The reality of unforgiveness is that it empowers people who wronged you, even if those people are no longer in your life. If you choose not to forgive someone, you are giving that person permission and a license to control your thoughts, your actions, and even your emotions. If you find yourself upset at the thought or mention of someone's name, then trust me: you have not forgiven that person.

Don't misunderstand me. I am not trying to minimize how you feel or the effects of someone else's hurtful choices on you personally and emotionally. I know that some people have a way of hurting you so badly that you think you won't ever recover. It is during those trying times that you need to lean on God even more.

Holding on to hurt closes us off to what God wants to do in our lives. When we study the parable of the prodigal son (Luke 15:11–32), more often than not, we hear the story of the son who left his father's house after demanding his inheritance. But I want to focus on the older brother. Although this brother stayed home, worked hard for his father, and served well, he was unforgiving and resentful of his younger brother. When the younger brother returned, the older brother all but screamed (in my words), "What about me? I did all this work, and now you throw him a party! Ain't that a trip?" In spite of everything he did that was good, he had resentment and bitterness in his heart instead of the joy and relief his father felt at being able to welcome his younger son home.

Unfortunately, the older brother became a willing victim. He saw his father's gift of reconciliation with the younger brother as a personal slight to him. No doubt he felt insulted, unappreciated, and rejected by the father he had served without interruption. As a result, he assumed a "holier than my brother" attitude when his father approached him about his absence from the party celebrating the younger brother's return.

Forgiveness requires bringing your feelings and thoughts into submission to God's word. In many cases, forgiveness requires confessing your desire to hold on to anger, resentment, and hostility toward a particular person. You have to ask yourself, "Why am I holding on to the hurt? What benefit am I getting from still being mad at this person?" Most often, it takes divine intervention to move you to a place where you know that the only way you can forgive someone who hurt you is with God's help.

Proverbs 18:19 describes a person who is so offended that he will not forgive. This scripture says, "A brother wronged is more unyielding than a fortified city; disputes are like the barred gates of a citadel" (NIV). Notice that the text compares someone who has been offended to an unyielding, fortified city. Unforgiveness causes people to be unyielding, inflexible, and unwilling to change. The only way to get into that fortified city is to come up with a military strategy to get past the walls.

Unforgiveness causes you to put up walls and be suspicious of everyone who comes into your life. If you are not careful, you may end up rejecting someone God is trying to send into your life, whether a potential mate, a friend, or a counselor.

KEEP ON FORGIVING

Forgiveness requires an attitude of humility and yielding to God, who commands us to forgive so that He can forgive our sins. Jesus said, "And when you stand praying, if you hold anything against anyone, forgive them, so that your Father in heaven may forgive you your sins" (Mark 11:25 NIV). You see, God knew that we would not forgive easily. He had to remind us that we "all have sinned and fall short of the glory of God" (Romans 3:23 NIV). If we expect and desire for God to forgive us, how can we withhold forgiveness from a brother or sister who needs it? Would we withhold our fellowship or a financial helping hand? Would we withhold from others the very things God has freely given us?

Another condition that God places on forgiveness is related to how many times we should forgive a person who sins against us. Peter asked Jesus, "Lord, how often shall my brother sin against me, and I forgive him? Up to seven times?" (Matthew 18:21 NKJV). We should consider the motive for asking this question. Did Peter really want to know the answer, or was he trying to justify not forgiving a particular person who wronged him repeatedly? Jesus said to Peter, "I do not say to you, up to seven times, but up to seventy times seven" (Matthew 18:22 NKJV).

I wonder if Peter was looking for an actual number or if he was trying to ask, "How long do I have to take this?" When Peter came to Jesus, what he was really saying, in our modern-day vernacular, was "How long do I have to put up with this craziness?" His motivation for asking the question was likely not forgiveness, but a desire for revenge. It is my opinion that Peter wanted to know how long he had to take the pain before he was justified in delivering a fleshly response.

Jesus' response that we should forgive someone "up to

seventy times seven" was not the answer Peter was looking for, because it forced him to rethink how long he should choose to hang on to an offense. Who would go through the trouble of keeping track of 490 offenses from a single person in order to feel justified in retaliating? Anyone who would do that has a bigger problem than the one that caused his or her pain.

Many people decide not to forgive, because they believe it would mean that the person who hurt them gets away with it. We must allow God to take care of our feelings of hurt, betrayal, and revenge (Psalm 147:3). We must also trust God to take care of the person who hurt us in whatever way He chooses (Romans 12:17–21).

Sometimes when I counsel couples, one of the spouses recounts offenses committed by the other in such detail and with such passion that I wonder if these incidents happened that week. When I ask about the timing of these offenses, I learn that they occurred years ago. Even though so much time has passed, the person is still clinging tightly to the hurt and can recount every detail of its origin. This is clearly a case of unresolved anger turning into bitterness and unforgiveness, and it needs to be dealt with. Without forgiveness, bitterness will ultimately destroy our relationships and ability to serve God effectively (Hebrews 12:15). It will put a marriage in hell and can be the cause of a marriage actually ending.

Jesus later had to teach Peter another lesson about forgiveness. Peter had no problem fighting, cursing, or cutting someone when he was questioned, felt attacked, or felt the need to defend Jesus. This was proven in the garden of

Gethsemane and in the three times Peter denied knowing Jesus (Matthew 26:47–54, 69–75; John 18:10–11). Jesus showed Peter that he needed Jesus' help to deal with his issues, and we, too, need His help. Jesus has to bring us to a place where we recognize and acknowledge our true selves and can see the ugliness, anger, and bitterness in our hearts. Jesus had to help Peter deal with his anger issues and emotional responses to his experiences in life. If Jesus had not helped Peter, he would never have been able to reach his full potential.

What unresolved issues are causing bitterness in your heart? Are there things or people you need to deal with before you can reach your destiny? Although Peter felt extremely embarrassed and ashamed about denying Jesus, he regained momentum and ultimately went on to do greater works. He did not sit around, crying about denying Jesus, beating himself up for his actions, or feeling sorry for himself. He knew he had been forgiven, and he took Jesus' restoration of him to heart.

A HEAVENLY VISION FOR MARRIAGE

It is important to understand what forgiveness is and what it is not. Forgiveness does not mean the immediate and complete restoration of trust. Imagine that someone comes to my house for a visit and steals something from my family, but before he gets home, the Lord convicts him of his wrongdoing. This person then returns to my house, confesses his sin, repents, and returns the item. What do you think I ought to do?

If you think I would immediately forgive this person, you are right, but don't get it twisted. I would immediately forgive this person for stealing from us and compromising our trust. However, it is highly unlikely that he would be invited back to our house anytime soon. Does that mean I have not forgiven him? No, I have forgiven him, but forgiveness does not mean the restoration of trust at the moment when the person asks for forgiveness. Trust takes seconds to lose but a long time to rebuild. That person would have to regain and earn back my trust before there could be a chance of the relationship being what it used to be.

Sometimes the relationship is never restored to what it was at the beginning, before the wrongdoing and the hurt. Sometimes relationships need to be redefined in order for the people involved to move forward and their relationship to grow. If you are going to have a marriage made in heaven, you cannot allow bitterness and resentment to rob you of your faith. You need to forgive your spouse so you can move forward together and build the relationship into what God intends it to be. You must have God at the center of your marriage and have a vision of what you want your marriage to be.

Proverbs 29:18 says, "Where there is no vision, the people perish: but he that keepeth the law, happy is he" (KJV). A successful marriage is one in which the couple has the vision to take the marriage where God wants it to go, not where the world or the individuals want it to go. *Vision* is defined as "the act or power of anticipating that which will or may come to be."[14] It is the ability to see an event vividly in your mind that has yet to happen in reality. Too often, people who have been hurt are looking in the rearview mirror rather than having a vision of how to forgive and make their marriage what it should be. Having this vision is critical to a successful marriage as well as a successful life in general.

Without this vision, marriage is like a swamp with no boundaries and no direction. However, with a clear, heavenly vision, a marriage is like a beautiful river. It has direction and is productive and full of life. Too many couples believe that marriage is a swamp to be tolerated instead of a river to be celebrated. God's plan all the way back to Adam and Eve shows us that marriage was meant to bless your life, not stress your life. Keeping track of old issues and carrying the baggage of unforgiveness weighs down your marriage when you should be seeking ways to uplift it.

Every relationship, including your relationship with God, needs to be continuously cultivated in order to reach its potential. A farmer cannot simply plant a crop and leave it alone, then go back in the fall and harvest a successful bounty. He has to continue to tend the crop, get rid of the weeds, and pray to God for blessings. It is the same with marriage. We have to get rid of the weeds and continue to nurture the relationship to make sure that the marriage grows into a heavenly one.

What I see with many believers is that the moment they experience a difficulty in the marriage (a weed), they allow the enemy to convince them that the situation will never change. The moment they buy into that lie, they become what I call "marital martyrs." In other words, they take on the mentality that they will suffer through the marriage for the sake of God's kingdom. They fail to realize that they could put that determination to better use if they would let God bring change in the marriage. The relationship does not have to stay where it is. Marriages are meant to grow and strengthen with the right tending.

You may be wondering, "Pastor, why do things like unforgiveness, adultery, and fornication happen in a marriage, even one of equally yoked Christians?" The enemy will always try to attack any family that is reaching its potential in God, because such a family is a model of God's relationship to the church. Please don't misunderstand. I am not saying that if you have a heavenly marriage and are doing God's will, that is a guarantee that you or your spouse is going to do something drastically wrong to harm the marriage. What I am saying is that the enemy will try to attack if given an opening to do so. The family needs to "put on the full armor of God" (Ephesians 6:10–18 NIV) and be ready to fight off the evil one.

The enemy does not have to waste time destroying the marriages of the ungodly. He already has them. I am convinced that he goes after the saved so he can use his evil ways to trap more unsuspecting victims. Always be on guard against the evil one and be sure that your marriage and family are built on the solid rock of God's word. You need to storm-proof your home, and God's word will give you the tools to do that.

TAKE RESPONSIBILITY FOR YOURSELF

Too often, we try to put all the blame on others and fail to look at ourselves. We look to others and wait for them to change. If the marriage is in hell because of any issue, perhaps you being the first to make a move to God and trust Him for restoration is the first step needed to navigate your marriage toward the heavenly vision you have in mind.

Recently, my wife and I were in Houston. I admit that when I am out of my comfort zone and in an unfamiliar area, I become directionally challenged. Therefore, each time I rent a car, I rent one that has a navigation system in it. Where we were, I had driven from the hotel to the church many times, but I still used the navigation system to get to my destination because I did not remember the names of the roads. One night, when we were on the way to the church service, the navigation system stopped working. My wife and I then struggled to get to our destination. We finally made it, but not without a great deal of stress and uncertainty.

I was angry and stressed. When I finally calmed down and thought it over, it became evident to me that the problem was not entirely the navigation system's fault. My trouble was caused because I was depending on something else to get me to my destination instead of taking responsibility for myself. It is the same with forgiveness. We must take responsibility for what is in our hearts that may be holding us back and choose to be the ones to make the first move. We must decide to live as God directs us if we are going to navigate through the swamps of life and see our vision of a heavenly marriage become a reality.

Chapter Eight Questions

Question: Consider a situation in which you have seen evidence of unforgiveness in a marriage. What were the effects of the unforgiveness on the couple and the family?

_____

_____

_____

_____

_____

_____

_____

_____

_____

_____

Question: Consider a situation in which you have seen evidence of a couple pursuing forgiveness after an offense. What was the outcome of these efforts?

_____

_____

_____

_____

_____

_____

_____

_____

Question: Have you ever been hurt by someone who was supposed to be your friend? How did you handle the situation?

_____

_____

_____

_____

_____

_____

_____

_____

_____

Question: Whose responsibility is forgiveness? Why is it important to forgive other people?

_____

_____

_____

_____

_____

_____

Action: You must be able to forgive yourself as well as others who have wronged you. Write on a piece of paper descriptions of at least five instances when you have been hurt or have hurt others. Now take the paper and shred it.

Action: Is there anyone you need to forgive? Is there anyone to whom you need to apologize? In either situation, if personal contact geared toward reconciliation is needed and possible, reach out to the person and arrange for a time to work through the situation.

Chapter Eight Notes

Ten Keys to a Heavenly Marriage

As we come to the close of this book on maximizing your marriage, I would like to leave you with ten practical points that, if taken to heart and lived on a daily basis, will help you to set your marriage on a heavenly course.

1. Commit to honesty and openness. Adam and Eve were naked in the garden of Eden (Genesis 2:25).

2. Communicate consistently with each other and with God. Men ought to be always in prayer.

3. Maintain a willingness to accept correction.

4. Be willing to admit when you are wrong and to repent of your sin.

5. Be willing to change. You must be willing to dethrone your flesh.

6. View marriage as a nonnegotiable commitment.

7. Give consistent praise to God (and encourage each

other as well).

8. If you quit moving for the better, it is at the risk of your personal happiness.

9. Press on toward maturity.

10. Stay committed to getting into the presence of God daily. This will give you the ability to tolerate and appreciate the presence of others and to see the blessings in the burdens.

As you put these measures and mindsets into practice, you will find that pursuing a heavenly marriage gives you an opportunity to see how legitimate your Christianity is. Everything it takes to be a good Christian is also an ingredient for a great marriage.

About the Author

Pastor John F. Ramsey, Sr., is the gifted and anointed founder and Senior Pastor of New Life Worship Center, an exciting and rapidly growing church located in Indianapolis, Indiana. He ministers with power while using humor to make often complex biblical concepts enjoyable, simple, relevant, and practical.

Pastor Ramsey attended Fort Wayne Public Schools and graduated from Snider High School. Following graduation, he accepted a football scholarship at Miami University of

Ohio and began pursuing a major in education. During his junior year, at the age of twenty-one, he accepted God's call to the ministry. It was during these college years that he began preparing himself to do God's will on a full-time basis.

In 2001, God called Pastor Ramsey and his wife, Alicia, to open the New Life Worship Center with the help of Eastern Star Church. Pastor Ramsey developed a central theme for New Life Worship Center: *"A Local Church with a Global Vision."* Pastor Ramsey and the New Life Worship Center family are fully positioned to reach God's people on a local, regional, national, and international scale.

As the worship center grew, it moved from its initial 350-seat sanctuary (Kessler location) to a new main location. In 2005, the worship center relocated to an 80,000-square-foot, 1,400-seat facility on thirteen acres in historic Trader's Point. Since its inception, the church has grown to over five thousand members, with thirty active ministries. In 2007, to serve the Indianapolis community more effectively, New Life Worship Center also completed the cash purchase of a central campus location at 3425 Boulevard Place in Center Township.

Pastor Ramsey serves as a mentor and spiritual father to a number of local pastors, and he is a member of the Association of Independent Ministries. He is blessed to serve under Bishop I. V. Hilliard of New Light Christian Center in Houston, Texas, as his spiritual father. Pastor Ramsey is a much sought-after preacher and a featured national keynote speaker for various leadership and development programs. God's anointing has enabled Pastor Ramsey to bring some of the nation's leading pastors, teachers, and recording artists to

New Life Worship Center to bless the congregation and the Indianapolis community each year. He is also a diversity consultant at Taylor University. He is part of the leadership team and serves as a ministry mentor.

Pastor Ramsey is most passionate about helping families to become stronger. Known for his anointing in the areas of faith, relationships, and financial stewardship, he is the author of *Smart Money Management*, *Armed and Dangerous*, *One Night Stand*, and *Money Before Marriage*. He is also the co-author of a highly regarded book entitled *About My Father's Business: Merging Industry and Ministry*.

Pastor Ramsey is married to his lovely wife, Alicia, and they are the proud parents of three wonderful children: daughter Judah Maree and sons Jeremiah David and John, Jr.

About Renown Publishing

WRITE YOUR BOOK & REDEEM CULTURE

Renown Publishing is the proud publishing imprint of Speak It To Book, an elite team of publishing professionals devoted to helping you shape, write, and share your book. Renown has written, edited, and worked on hundreds of books (including New York Times, Wall Street Journal, and USA Today best-sellers, and the #1 book on all of Amazon).

We believe authentic stories are the torch of change-makers, and our mission is to collaborate with purpose-driven authors to create societal impact and redeem culture.

If you're the founder of a purpose-driven company, visit RenownPublishing.com.

If you're an aspiring author, visit SpeakItToBook.com.

Notes

1. Lee, Esther. "This Was the Average Age of Marriage in 2021." The Knot. February 15, 2022. https://www.theknot.com/content/average-age-of-marriage#:~:text=In%202021%2C%20the%20average%20age,the refore%20falls%20at%2034%20years.

2. Lee, "This Was the Average Age of Marriage in 2021."

3. Ballard, Jamie. "Do Americans Believe in the Idea of Soulmates?" YouGovAmerica. February 10, 2021. https://today.yougov.com/topics/lifestyle/articles-reports/2021/02/10/soulmates-poll-survey-data.

4. Wilkinson and Finkbeiner Family Law Attorneys. "Divorce Statistics: Over 115 Studies, Facts and Rates for 2022." https://www.wf-lawyers.com/divorce-statistics-and-facts/#:~:text=60%20percent%20 of%20couples%20married,less%20likely%20to%20get%20divorced.

5. Wilkinson and Finkbeiner, "Divorce Statistics."

6. Menasce Horowitz, Juliana, Nikki Graf, and Gretchen Livingston. "Marriage and Cohabitation in the U. S." Pew Research Center. November 6, 2019. https://www.pewresearch.org/social-trends/2019/

11/06/marriage-and-cohabitation-in-the-u-s/.

7. Rosenfeld, Michael J., and Kathrina Roesler. "Cohabitation Experience and Cohabitation's Association with Marital Dissolution." *Journal of Marriage and Family* 81, no. 1 (February 2019): p. 42–58. https://doi.org/10.1111/jomf.12530.

8. Wilkinson and Finkbeiner, "Divorce Statistics."

9. Stanley, Thomas J. *The Millionaire Mind*. RosettaBooks, 2010.

10. Stigler, Kimberly A., and Christopher J. McDougle. "Structural and Functional MRI Studies of Autism Spectrum Disorders." Chapter 3 in *The Neuroscience of Autism Spectrum Disorders*. Edited by Joseph D. Buxbaum and Patrick R. Hof. Academic Press, 2012, p. 255.

11. Dictionary.com, "adultery." https://www.dictionary.com/browse/adultery.

12. Merriam-Webster Online Dictionary, "lust." merriam-webster.com/dictionary/lust.

13. Merriam-Webster Online Dictionary, "temptation." https://www.merriam-webster.com/dictionary/temptation.

14. Dictionary.com, "vision." https://www.dictionary.com/browse/vision.